Private Affairs

SEXUAL CULTURES: New Directions from the Center for Lesbian and Gay Studies

General Editors: José Esteban Muñoz and Ann Pellegrini

Times Square Red, Times Square Blue
Samuel R. Delany

Private Affairs
Critical Ventures in the Culture of Social Relations
Phillip Brian Harper

Private Affairs

Critical Ventures in the Culture of Social Relations

PHILLIP BRIAN HARPER

NEW YORK UNIVERSITY PRESS
New York and London

NEW YORK UNIVERSITY PRESS
New York and London

Library of Congress Cataloging-in-Publication Data
Harper, Phillip Brian.
Private affairs : critical ventures in the culture of social relations / Phillip Brian Harper.
p. cm. — (Sexual cultures : new directions from the Center for Gay and Lesbian Studies)
Includes bibliographical references and index.
ISBN 0-8147-3593-2 (cloth : acid-free paper)
ISBN 0-8147-3594-0 (pbk. : acid-free paper)
1. Privacy, Right of. 2. Interpersonal relations and culture.
3. Privacy. 4. Minorities—Civil rights. I. Title. II. Series.
JC596 .H37 1999
323.44'8—dc21 99-6005
CIP

New York University Press books are printed on acid-free paper, and their binding materials are chosen for strength and durability.

Manufactured in the United States of America
10 9 8 7 6 5 4 3 2 1

for Thom, in eager anticipation

Contents

Preface

On the night of Monday, August 17, 1998, President Bill Clinton delivered a televised address to the nation during which he admitted that, contrary to what he had asserted over the preceding seven months, he did have a relationship with Monica Lewinsky—presumably during the period in the mid 1990s when she was a twenty-one-year-old unpaid White House intern—and that that relationship was "not appropriate."[1] Rather than belaboring—or even elaborating—this point in his remarks, however, the president instead used the speech as an occasion to denounce the investigation into his activities then being conducted by independent counsel Kenneth W. Starr, and, in particular, to assert as rightfully ineligible for investigative scrutiny the "private life" to which a sitting president, no less than the rest of the citizenry, is fundamentally entitled.

Indeed, having been invoked a total of seven times in an address that clocked in at well under five minutes, *privacy* would seem to constitute not only the chief focus of the president's remarks in the particular instance but also the primary conceptual and discursive category through which what is essential to the life of the nation is differentiated from that which has no bearing upon it. Clinton himself recurred to precisely this distinction when he urged that we "get on with our national life" as opposed to "the pursuit of personal destruction and the prying into private lives" with which the Starr investigation had "distracted" the country's attention. But of course, if it were possible for personal behavior to be rendered functionally irrelevant to national interest by virtue merely of presidential decree, then we would not have seen the number of military personnel discharged on grounds of homosexuality increase by 67 percent in the three years following the 1994 implementation of the infamous "don't ask, don't tell, don't pursue" policy[2]—a development that indicates the degree to which privacy is contested in settings far removed from the halls of state power, the president's suggestion to the contrary notwithstanding. For by insisting that "even Presidents have private lives"—and thus implying that, practically speaking, the presidency actually *lacks* the benefits of privacy—Clinton managed to conceive the latter as the signal privilege of ordinary citizens, for whom it remains unproblematically inviolate so long as they do not voluntarily, altruistically, assume the responsibilities of public office (or mass-cultural celebrity, for that matter) and the burden of constant examination such service unfortunately entails.

This understanding of the situation may in fact be accurate to the extent that by "ordinary" we mean not only obscure but socially *normative* and thus not discernibly threatening to the maintenance of the cultural status quo. From the second a person manifests a *non*-normative behavior or attribute in which is located the basis for a minoritized identity, however—which for some of us in the U.S. context is from the second we are born—the protection of privacy to which President Clinton so wistfully alluded is withdrawn with a decisiveness that would seem to exceed that of any judgment the chief executive could suffer.

By this I mean that many members of the population who diverge from social norms—the person who engages in same-sex eroticism, the individual who immigrates from another country, the nonwhite citizen, the poor person—thereby become assimilable to specific classes that are systematically subjected to intense regulatory scrutiny; and, further, that the flip side of blessed obscurity characteristically entails a lack of the resources necessary to defend against such surveillance even were it acknowledged to constitute a potential invasion of privacy, whereas the very terms of President Clinton's address indicated that he actually enjoys extensive access to such resources, which themselves might be construed as aspects of the privacy whose loss he was suggesting he faced. The various references to privacy that Clinton made during his speech bore somewhat disparate significances, after all. Focused most consistently on the sacrosanct—because personally *intimate*—character of his sexual and familial relations, these references seemed additionally to implicate activities of the president that are merely hidden from public view (Clinton affirmed his responsibility for "all my actions, both public and private"), as well as undertakings that are neither personally intimate nor socially invisible in their meanings and effects. Even before explicitly asserting that the Starr investigation had gone on "for too long," the president indicated that he had experienced qualms about the inquiry from the beginning because it had been targeted initially at "private business dealings 20 years ago." This allusion to his and Hillary Rodham Clinton's involvement in the Whitewater investment plan points up Bill Clinton's enjoyment of assets comprised in—as well as influence deriving from—*private property*, such that his standing within the larger society is clearly rooted in more than electoral popularity per se, especially inasmuch as the latter itself extends from those assets—and that influence—in the first place. If this private wealth also connotes the wherewithal to mount a defense of one's private *life*—including the interpersonal relations partly constituting it—then that fact simply shows that these two powerfully resonant modes of privacy are mutually supportive in their routine social effects, however much their interrelation may be concealed in official cultural discourses.

By the late 1980s it had been made quite clear that certain constituencies in the United States do not enjoy the access to personal privacy that President Clinton suggested is a well-nigh universally held right—or even to the family formation in which such privacy is conventionally located and to which Clinton himself pointedly took recourse in his remarks about his relationship with Monica Lewinsky, declaring his determination "to reclaim my family life for my family"; the Sharon Kowalski custody case in Wisconsin (discussed in "Private Affairs," presented below) and the even more notorious 1986 Supreme Court decision in *Bowers v. Hardwick* both demonstrated that persons involved in homosexual relations cannot count on the privacy protection that all U.S. citizens are putatively able to take for granted. Less salient to popular consciousness, however, was the extent to which certain U.S. populations had historically been denied the right to *proprietary privacy* that is instanced in the president's business dealings, and the degree to which constraints on the one mode of privacy actually derived from concerns about limiting access to the other. This limit on access to proprietary privacy had, of course, been suffered most intensely by black people existing in slavery before the Civil War, whose right to hold property was rendered problematic, to say the least, by the fact that they themselves constituted *objects* of property. Considering the relatively long—albeit understandably troubled—history of lesbian and gay activists' recurrence to black–civil rights struggles for cues on how to advance a comparable movement, I decided in about 1989 that it would be worthwhile to interrogate the social-structural principles underlying the two types of minority experience, and consequently set about trying to get at these through the mode of engaged cultural analysis that I felt best equipped to pursue.

The immediate result was the title essay of this volume; the more significant consequence was my embarkation on an extended inquiry into the varied ways in which privacy figures in contemporary U.S. culture and society. Working on what strikes me as the well-founded understanding that social-minority status, in particular, forcefully shows up the general effects of privacy—whether construed in terms of self and psyche, interpersonal relations, property rights, or various combinations thereof—I proceeded over the course of the subsequent decade to investigate a number of key sociocultural moments in which privacy claims seemed to give way under the pressures of minoritized experience. Having traced racial and sexual minority statuses as relatively distinct—if interrelated—social modes in "Private Affairs," I went on in "'The Subversive Edge'" to consider how the two modes conjoin within certain subjects' experiences so as to limit severely their exercise of control over even their personal images, which constitute objects of both personal and proprietary privacy. By focusing in this essay on the experiences of the queens featured in the widely admired and extensively acclaimed documentary film *Paris Is Burning*, I sought to correct what struck me as a general misapprehension regarding the queens' capacity, through their admittedly potent camp performances, actually to intervene substantively in the larger social field.

Conversely, in "Playing in the Dark," I attempted to demonstrate that the terms by which privacy—and, key here, *publicity*—is constituted within the larger social field are so elastic as to be able to impinge upon and regulate subjects not even engaged in conscious socially-directed activity. Taking putatively "public sex" as its primary object of examination (being conceived as it was in the aftermath of actor Paul "Pee-wee Herman" Reubens's 1991 arrest for indecent exposure), this piece inaugurated my use of the personal anecdote as a central analytical strategy, meant to discover the quotidian effects of social structures and cultural formations all too often conceived as "merely" theoretical. This anecdotal approach was incorporated along with a number of other critical methodologies in the essay "Gay Male Identities, Personal Privacy, and Relations of Public Exchange," in which I tried to detail the similarly varied—and highly complex—ways in which gay male identity can be registered in contemporary U.S. culture, with a wide range of potential consequences, depending upon how easily any given gay male subject can manipulate the terms of privacy and publicity through which gayness is made sense of in the extended social field.

Personal anecdote finally becomes central in "'Take Me Home,'" which seeks to reckon with recent demands for a transnational U.S. cultural analysis by disclosing the extent to which native-born U.S. citizens might actually live their transnationalism in emphatically *nationalist* modes, even when that lived experience is registered in the highly privatized domain of the personal psyche. Foregrounding issues of citizenship and socioeconomic class, the essay considers these in relation to the matters of racial and sexual identity that predominate in the other pieces, thereby opening for further consideration the question of how such aspects of identity variously figure in the diverse range of situations in which they come into play. If these essays, which make up the bulk of the volume, indicate how discrete moments in recent history and in personal life are imbued with significance relating to conceptions of privacy, then the afterword, like this preface, is meant to suggest how that significance extends even into the "national life" that President Clinton tried mightily to distinguish from properly private affairs and thus is of ongoing concern for those of us interested in the workings of contemporary U.S. culture and society.

Each of the essays presented here is marked with a date or dates indicating the time of its first drafting and/or its initial publication. The purpose of this is both to situate the analyses in relation to the specific occasions to which they were meant to respond, and to suggest how my own thinking about privacy—with all its faults and inadequacies—has developed over the course of the past ten years. The range of sites in which some of the work collected in this volume has already appeared—often in slightly different versions than follow below—itself signals the extent to which privacy is of serious interest for intellectuals working in a variety of fields, and so it may be particularly helpful to review this publication history here. "Private Affairs" first appeared in 1994 in *GLQ: A Journal of Lesbian and Gay Studies,* and again in the volume *Professions of Desire: Lesbian and Gay Studies in Literature,* edited by George E. Haggerty and Bonnie Zimmerman, pp. 210–32 (New York: Modern Language Association Publications, 1995); copyright © 1995 The Modern Language Association of America, New York. "'The Subversive Edge'" was published in *Critical Crossings,* a special double issue of *diacritics* (24.2–3; Summer/Fall 1994), edited by Judith Butler and Biddy Martin, pp. 90–103; copyright © 1994 The Johns Hopkins University Press. "Playing in the Dark" was published in 1994 in issue number 30 of *Camera Obscura: A Journal of Feminism and Film Theory* (May 1992; issued June 1994), pp. 93–111; copyright © 1992 Indiana University Press. "Gay Male Identities, Personal Privacy, and Relations of Public Exchange" appeared in *Queer Transexions of Race, Nation, and Gender,* a special double issue of *Social Text* 52/53 (15.3–4; Fall/Winter 1997), edited by Phillip Brian Harper, Anne McClintock, José Esteban Muñoz, and Trish Rosen, pp. 5–29; copyright © 1997 Duke University Press. I am grateful to the editors of *Camera Obscura,* to the Modern Language Association, and to the Johns Hopkins, Duke, and Indiana University Presses for permission to reprint these essays here.

As is suggested above, the analyses in this volume are elements in a long-term investigation of privacy in which I am still engaged. I am very fortunate to have the benefit of a number of friends who continue to help me grapple with the topic, and who have aided me in producing the work collected here by reading and commenting on drafts of the various pieces, sponsoring lectures in which I first presented ideas elaborated therein, or publishing sections of the book in their earlier versions. The roster of these supportive colleagues includes Henry Abelove, Gerard Aching, Jonathan Arac, Michael Awkward, Judith Butler, Douglas Crimp, Carolyn Dever, Carolyn Dinshaw, Lisa Duggan, Lee Edelman, David Eng, Shelly Eversley, Leyla Ezdinli, Jonathan Flatley, Judith Frank, Elizabeth Freeman, Diana Fuss, Joshua Gamson, Marjorie Garber, George Haggerty, David Halperin, Barbara Johnson, Miranda Joseph, Rosemary Kegl, Joe Litvak, Biddy Martin, Anne McClintock, Kobena Mercer, Sylvia Molloy, Adam Zachary Newton, Jeff Nunokawa, Ricardo Ortíz, Cindy Patton, Don Pease, Constance Penley, Mary Poovey, Claire Potter, Robert Reid-Pharr, Amy Robinson, Trish Rosen, Lynne Segal, Nayan Shah, Chris Straayer, Sasha Torres, Rebecca Walkowitz, Patricia White, Robyn Wiegman, Sharon Willis, Marilyn Young, and Bonnie Zimmerman. Many of those listed above have been participants in the Faculty Working Group in Queer Studies that has met at New York University for the past five years or so, which has been invaluable in the development of my thinking about the issues addressed here. José Esteban Muñoz and Ann Pellegrini, in addition to serving in the capacities noted above, have been especially helpful in their role as editors of the series in which this volume appears. My editor at New York University Press, Eric Zinner, has been a model of support, wisdom, and intellectual perspicacity, as he always is; and press staffer Daisy Hernández handled the intricacies of production with remarkable skill and good humor. Brian Johnson provided expert photographic services; and Mabel Wilson and Carlos Decena rendered crucial research assistance, with the latter also proofreading the book, along with Patrick McCreery, with exemplary care and efficiency. Finally, Thom Freedman, to whom the volume is dedicated, sustains me in ways beyond my ability to articulate; luckily for me, and as I hope he agrees, it isn't necessary that I succeed in that here.

P.B.H.

New York City
November 1998

Notes

1. The full text of the president's notably brief speech was reprinted the next day in, among other publications, the *New York Times* (18 August 1998: A12).

2. Jennifer Egan, "Uniforms in the Closet," *New York Times Magazine,* 28 June 1998: 26+; cited from The New York Times ® Ondisc, paragraph eight.

For a characteristically trenchant analysis of the circumstances under which the "don't ask, don't tell, don't pursue" policy was adopted, see Janet E. Halley, "The Status/Conduct Distinction in the 1993 Revisions to Military Anti-Gay Policy: A Legal Archaeology," *GLQ: A Journal of Lesbian and Gay Studies* 3.2–3 (1996): 159–252.

1 Private Affairs

Race, Sex, Property, and Persons

The Kiss

I begin this inquiry into the social significances of privacy in what may seem an unlikely manner, by examining some recent critical commentary on modern European painting and sculpture. Specifically, I want to consider discussions of works by Auguste Rodin, Constantin Brancusi, and Gustav Klimt, who, for all their differences in choices of media and technique, share at least one title, which designates one or more of each one's best-known works. I am referring, of course, to *The Kiss*. Each artist's rendition of "the kiss" is, to be sure, stylistically distinctive, but as the commonality of the title suggests, all the works nonetheless develop the same theme, depicting a male and a female figure engaged in both a full embrace and the aforementioned kiss. The stylistic variation among the works has led critics to assert that each of them has a unique effect. And yet the language in which these assertions are couched suggests more congruence among the different conceptions of the kiss than is generally acknowledged in the literature. Indeed, it would seem that one particular formulation of the kiss's cultural significance has achieved such hegemony as to make it ripe for the interrogation that I want to pursue here.

Let us consider, for example, Bernard Champigneulle's description of Rodin's sculpture *The Kiss* (1886) as "that luminous symbol of love and of the twofold tenderness of man the protector and woman stirred to the depths of her being."[1] What is, perhaps, most familiar in this assessment is the positing of the male figure as imperturbably stolid (in his protectiveness) even as he acts upon the female in such a way that she, by contrast, is utterly moved. The degree to which this particular conception of heterosexual communion has been thoroughly stereotyped is best indicated by its pervasiveness in both soft- and hard-core pornography, in which the pleasure that is supposed to characterize the sexual encounter is generally registered through the woman's groans and facial expressions while the man, despite his customary energy and athleticism, appears comparatively unaffected. Notably, Champigneulle does not actually identify the characteristics of the sculpture that indicate to him the subjects' emotional states (and, frankly, I cannot discern them myself); instead, his claim acquires its plausibility through its recourse to representational conventions of the heterosexual relation with which we are extensively familiar.

At the same time that he notes the different moods of the two figures, however, Champigneulle also comments on their formal continuity with one another; "[f]rom lips to feet," he remarks, "both figures are pervaded by the same fluidity" (157). It is in the interplay between this continuity, on the one hand, and the distinction of masculine and feminine sensibilities, on the other, that we can identify the basis for the characteristic conception of the heterosexual coupling as the necessary overcoming of a fundamen-

Auguste Rodin, *The Kiss,* 1886.

tal difference between the genders—a conception that is reflected in much of the critical commentary on Rodin's sculpture. For instance, having noted the "incredulous" critical reaction to the stolid "reticence" of *The Kiss*'s male figure, Albert E. Elsen goes on to suggest that that incredulity might be quelled by the sculptural "fusion" of male and female that Rodin elsewhere achieves, thereby clearly indicating the degree to which such fusion is considered "natural" to the heterosexual encounter—construed as a convergence of polarities—whose teleological imperative of union is represented in the kiss itself.[2]

This postulation of the heterosexual kiss's significance as the overcoming of gendered difference also marks commentary on the work of the Romanian-born French sculptor Constantin Brancusi. Brancusi completed numerous versions of his own *Kiss*, most in stone, and according to Sidney Geist, all of these represent "the antithesis of *The Kiss* of Rodin" in their frank abstractionism.[3] Nevertheless, Geist's analysis implicates Brancusi's work in the same conception of the kiss's import that informs Champigneulle's commentary on Rodin. Geist begins his examination of one of Brancusi's earliest versions of the work, from about 1907–1908, by noting that the "two lovers . . . are eye to eye, their lips mingle, the breasts of the woman encroach gently on the form of the man" (28). He goes on to stress the merged quality of the two figures—"[t]he unity of the bodies"—but finds fault with their arms, whose "round, ropelike *separable* character . . . violates the continuity of the stony matter" (28, emphasis in original). This violation is repaired, according to Geist, in a more columnar version of *The Kiss* done in 1909, which presents the two figures with full bodies, "the legs of the woman embrac[ing] those of the man" (36). This *Kiss*, Geist claims, "accomplishes the weaving of forms without destroying the integrity of the stone"; and by thus manifesting such formal continuity the later work, Geist asserts, "marks an advance . . . over the

Constantin Brancusi, *The Kiss,* 1907–8 (Craiova). Copyright © 1999 ARS, New York/ADAGP, Paris.

Constantin Brancusi, *The Kiss,* 1909 (Montparnasse Cemetery). Copyright © 1999 ARS, New York/ADAGP, Paris.

first *Kiss*" (36). We are, it seems, meant to apprehend the extent of that advance from Geist's assessment that Brancusi's "image of two figures locked in an embrace is a permanent expression of the unity of love, which Plato called 'the desire and pursuit of the whole'" (37).

In the conjunction of Geist's privileging of the "pursuit of the whole" that is evidently figured in the heterosexual union, and his enthusiasm for Brancusi's abstractionist aesthetic (which is discernible throughout his essay), we can identify a dichotomy similar to that which characterizes the Rodin criticism: formal continuity set against emotional distance. Moreover, in his anxiety to render this schema in clearly heterosexual terms, Geist actually seems to betray his own modernist ethic by insisting that *The Kiss*'s representation of heterosexual union is based not only in realism but, further, in biography. In his assessment of the earlier *Kiss*, Geist notes the peculiarities of the two different figures in the sculpture:

> *The man's hair falls over his brow, much as Brancusi wore [his] in 1904. The line of the hair starts at a higher point on the woman, giving her a somewhat longer face than the man, and making her appear slightly taller (and Brancusi was short). It is reasonable to speculate that this carving . . . celebrates a consummated kiss. If it does, we must conclude that what seems to be a set of formal variations has a biographical origin. (29)*

And, in his commentary on what is arguably Brancusi's best-known version of *The Kiss*, done in 1912, Geist implicitly faults the sculpture for "los[ing] the immediacy of the earlier versions as it moves toward pure design" (40). Thus Geist's celebration of Brancusi's modernist aesthetic, which he prizes for its "timelessness, simplicity and autonomy" (28), is mitigated by his uneasy desire to assimilate the sculpture to a narrative of recognizably heterosexual love in which the kiss must be the inevitable "consummation." Indeed, when the work is so abstract as to

Constantin Brancusi, *The Kiss*, 1912 (Philadelphia Museum of Art). Copyright © 1999 ARS, New York/ADAGP, Paris.

Constantin Brancusi, *Medallion,* c. 1919 (Musée National d'Art Moderne, Paris). Copyright © 1999 ARS, New York/ ADAGP, Paris.

present figures that are barely differentiated, even, let alone gendered—thus rendering impossible this sort of heterosexual recuperation—Geist is forced to desperate measures. Considering the presentation of the kiss in *Medallion,* from around 1919, Geist negotiates the potential for distress that is implicated in the figures' unisexual appearance by construing those figures as not human but, rather, immortal. This version of the work, he says, "echoes Donne: 'Difference of sex no more we knew than our guardian angels do'" (80–81); he thus casts the carving's lack of gender differentiation in terms of angelic purity rather than human decadence.

While Geist may appear singularly ingenious in his management of the more troubling aspects of Brancusi's various *Kiss*es, however, so potent and versatile is the mythology of heterosexual love that the dichotomous impulse it animates in Geist's consideration of Brancusi's work might be incorporated into a completely different interpretational scheme without in the least forfeiting its ultimate significance. In his study of the work of Austrian artist Gustav Klimt, Frank Whitford notes the contemporaneity of Brancusi's sculpture and Klimt's famous painting *The Kiss* (1908), claiming that

to compare them is to see instantly the differences between Klimt's work and that of another, more completely modern artist. . . . [W]hereas Brancusi sim-

plifies, reduces and rarefies, Klimt complicates, allows his ornament to proliferate and adds layer after layer of effect and allusion.[4] *(118)*

In short, as a less "modern" artist, Klimt is less abstract in his work than Brancusi, and thus Klimt's painting needs less to be reclaimed by a realistic narrative of heterosexual love than it needs, on the contrary, to be rescued from an overly specific interpretation derived from autobiographical realism. Consequently, while Geist underscores the extent to which Brancusi's *Kiss* can be traced to the artist's own experiences and thus presumably reinvested with the heterosexual significance that it is always threatening to lose through its high abstraction, Whitford denies the biographical significance of Klimt's painting (the heterosexual meaning of which is relatively clear) in order to claim that the work registers the "universality" of the love it apparently treats:

In some of the preliminary drawings the man is depicted with a beard and it has therefore inevitably been suggested that the male figure is Klimt himself and the woman an idealized portrait of Adele Bloch-Bauer, whose affair with Klimt was supposedly continuing when The Kiss *was painted. The only evidence for this, however, is the awkward position of the woman's right hand [Adele Bloch-Bauer had an anomalously configured right hand] (but this masks the fourth, and not the disfigured middle finger). The painting is not autobiographical but a symbolic, universalized statement about sexual love. (118)*

What Whitford takes as "universal" about the depiction, it would seem, is the notion (which the painting apparently espouses) that the kiss represents the logical end of the heterosexual encounter—a notion explicitly evidenced in the title of a forerunner to *The Kiss*, Klimt's *Fulfillment* (1905–9), which depicts a scene very similar to that presented in the later work. (One notable difference, according

Gustav Klimt, *The Kiss,* 1908 (Oesterreichische Galerie, Vienna). Erich Lessing/Art Resource, New York.

to Whitford, is that in *The Kiss,* "the woman's ecstasy . . . [is] revealed in her face" (117), just as I have suggested is usual in representations of heterosexual erotic pairing.) It is necessary, I think, to examine critically this very notion, for if we view the kiss merely as emblematizing the consummation of heterosexual love, we miss its import in other social contexts; at the same time, it is necessary to recognize the extent to which that consummation is taken to be the primary significance of the kiss before we can fully appreciate its meaning in the other economies of signification that I want to consider here.

If, as I have suggested is indicated in the art criticism discussed above, the kiss is generally understood to signify the logical consummation of the heterosexual encounter, then, conversely, any rela-

Gustav Klimt, *Fulfillment,* detail of the *Beethoven Frieze,* 1905–9 (Oesterreichische Galerie, Vienna). Erich Lessing/Art Resource, New York.

tionship between a man and a woman that registers as "heterosexual" must be considered as founded on an erotic charge that is "hidden" beneath the relationship's day-to-day aspect, and that achieves public expression in the kiss. The kiss, then, in teleologically "fulfilling" that relationship, retroactively invests with an inevitably erotic significance all the interactions that have heretofore constituted the relationship. Further, because the notion that the sexualized encounter does ineluctably comprise such a telos is so strong a force in Western culture, we are able to "know" that any recognizably heterosexual relation "really" represents an erotic engagement, however "innocent" of eroticism the constituent interactions in that relation may appear to be. The status of the properly heterosexual relation, then, is always that of the "open secret," the revelation of which (through the publicized kiss, for example) will startle us only because, as D. A. Miller has pointed out, "[w]e too inevitably surrender our privileged position as readers to whom all secrets are open by 'forgetting' our knowledge for the pleasures of suspense and surprise."[5] Miller invokes "readers" because he is discussing specifically our experience of novelistic narrative. Yet "reading" seems an apt description of our activity as decoders of social texts as well as fictional ones. After all, as Miller indicates, "the social function of secrecy [is] isomorphic with its novelistic function," and that function is "not to conceal knowledge, so much as to conceal the knowledge of the knowledge" (206). The necessity for this concealment, in Miller's assessment, derives from a subject's desire to disavow the degree to which he or she has been absorbed and accounted for in the social totality he or she inhabits. That is to say that secrecy serves as a sort of "defense mechanism" by which, as Miller puts it,

the subject is allowed to conceive of himself as a resistance: a friction in the smooth functioning of the social order. . . . [It is] the subjective practice in which the oppositions of private/public, inside/outside, subject/object are established, and the sanctity of their first term kept inviolate. (207)

What secrecy accomplishes, then (to focus on the first of the oppositions Miller lists), is the very creation of the notion of privacy. That notion is operative, obviously, in the epistemology of the heterosexual relation—as is suggested by the points I have already made regarding it; but it is also a crucial category (just as the kiss is a signal phenomenon) in realms that are far more socially and politically troublesome, to which I would like now to turn.

Who's Afraid of Miscegenation?

Owing to their presumed basis in personal emotions, which are themselves considered to be essentially internal to our psychic mechanisms, interpersonal relations are conventionally seen as thoroughly comprised in the private realm, denoting a site of unconstrained personal choice and agency. Nonetheless, we need not look far to find instances in which that realm—and the social interactions presumed to take place therein—has been regulated either by the state or by some other entity external to the private sphere. Indeed, it is precisely when such putatively private matters as interpersonal relations become subject to external regulation that their sanctity is most likely to be defensively invoked. The African-American writer Frances Ellen Watkins Harper presents a prime example of such an invocation in her 1892 novel, *Iola Leroy*.

The title character of Harper's novel, which is set during the Civil War and the ensuing period of Reconstruction, is a young woman of "mixed blood"—specifically, the daughter of a wealthy white planter from the Mississippi delta and a white-skinned octoroon woman who had been the planter's slave before the two of them fell in love and were married. Iola and her brother, Harry, have been raised to believe that they are of purely European heritage, and they are disabused of this notion only after their father, Eugene, dies, and his evil cousin remands them and their mother, Marie, to slavery. Following a fortuitous confluence of events, Iola escapes from bondage to work as a nurse in the camps of the Union army during the war. While there, she meets Dr. Gresham, a white physician from New England who falls in love with her and requests her hand in marriage repeatedly over the years, even after he learns the secret of her racial heritage. At the final proposal, Iola informs Dr. Gresham that, despite his affection, there exists an "insurmountable barrier" between them. When he asks what it is, she replies, "It is the public opinion which assigns me a place with the colored people." Unconvinced, Dr. Gresham marshals the argument of privacy to which I have already alluded: "[W]hat right," he demands, "has public opinion to interfere with our marriage relations?"[6] Iola notes that she and Dr. Gresham are constrained to conform to public opinion because "it is stronger than we are" (231), and she might add that that strength derives largely from legal authority because popular antimiscegenation sentiment was encoded in laws prohibiting interracial marriage and sexual relations in some states well into the twentieth century.[7]

Thus the boundary between the public and the private realms is not so impermeable as it has often been taken to be. This is not a new revelation: a whole tradition of feminist critique, along with other schools of social theory, has already called into question the public/private dichotomy.[8] What I want to focus on here, however, is how the public/private distinction (and its problematic character) is actually inscribed not only in relations between different social subjects but also in individual subjects themselves, and this in such a way as to complicate profoundly the very constitution of minority identity.

A prime character through which to interrogate these issues is Iola Leroy herself, since her status as a white-skinned Negro situates her on the line that distinguishes public from private in conventional assessments. By this I mean that the very existence not only of Iola, but of the light-skinned Negro *generally*, destabilizes the conventional link between socially constituted racial identity and the apparent biological fact of skin color. Indeed, since Iola's skin color does not correspond to her racial identification (once she learns of her Negro "blood," Iola fully identifies with black people), that racial identification remarkably takes on the status of a secret—one whose revelation will always come as a shock precisely because it disrupts the standard association between skin color and racial identity. The fundamentally *private* nature of Iola's racial identification is made clear in a key passage from Harper's novel. After a series of amazing coincidences that serve to reunite her with her mother, her brother, and her uncle once the war is over, Iola decides to seek employment in the northern locale where she has settled. She is twice disappointed in her efforts when her fellow employees at the stores where she finds work as a saleswoman learn that she is actually a Negro. Nonetheless, as she tells her Uncle Robert,

> *"I am determined to win for myself a place in the fields of labor. I have heard of a place in New England, and I mean to try for it, even if I only stay a few months."*
>
> *"Well, if you* will *go, say nothing about your color."*
>
> *"Uncle Robert, I see no necessity for proclaiming that fact on the housetop. Yet I am resolved that nothing shall tempt me to deny it. The best blood in my veins is African blood, and I am not ashamed of it." (208)*

Note that Robert specifically enjoins Iola not to say anything about her *color*. This choice of words is not a slip, for the term *color* is conventionally used as a euphemism for racial identification. Iola's case demonstrates particularly well the problems with this usage, however; Iola's actual skin color, which is visible to anyone who looks at her, needs no explanation unless the secret of her Negro identification is revealed, and it is this disclosure that Robert is actually warning her against. Thus racial identification, which is normally taken to be a matter of public knowledge, is for Iola actually a *private* matter the publication of which will extensively affect her private life, including, as we have seen, her personal relations, such as her attachment with Dr. Gresham.

Iola's story shares some key elements with the narrative that I have suggested informs the critical commentary on Rodin, Brancusi, and Klimt, which I will call the narrative of the standard heterosexual relation. These elements include a social existence that is bifurcated into public and private realms, and an affective attachment whose relation to those realms is complex and problematic. In the narrative of the standard heterosexual relation, that attachment is represented in the kiss; in *Iola Leroy* it is constituted by the romantic overtures of Dr. Gresham. The contextual specificities—or lack thereof—presented in the two narratives, however, dictate distinctive functions and significances for these elements in each instance. In the standard heterosexual narrative, the fundamentally erotic character of the relationship between the key figures is exposed by the culminatory kiss, which thus simultaneously confirms our knowledge of that relationship's primary "secret"; in Iola's case, on the other hand, the revelation of the secret—which here has to do with racial identification—works a transformation upon the affective attachment (and in the rest of Iola's "private" life as well) that prevents its being erotically "fulfilled" in the manner prescribed in the narrative of the standard heterosexual relation.

This interruption of the relationship's erotic trajectory is figured in the novel when Dr. Gresham, faced with Iola's suggestion that any children they might produce could show "unmistakable signs of color," seriously reconsiders his marriage proposal (117). Such a break constitutes only one possible outcome of the revelation of Iola's secret, however—just one possible manifestation of the change in her personal relations effected by that disclosure—for, paradoxically and tellingly, that revelation can also actually *precipitate* an erotic assay, given the peculiar sociosexual regime obtaining in the United States during the period in which Iola's story is set. Indeed, Harper's novel offers a vivid instance of such an occurrence, which takes place before Iola herself has become aware of her racial status.

Once Iola's father dies, his cousin, Alfred Lorraine, sends two envoys, named Camille and Bastine, to the North, where Iola is enrolled in a private boarding school. Their mission is to trick her into returning to the South with them so that she can be sold into slavery before she actually learns either that her father is dead or that she is legally considered to be a Negro. While the party is waiting between trains in a large Southern hotel, Iola drifts off to sleep:

> *In her dreams she was at home, encircled in the warm clasp of her father's arms, feeling her mother's kisses lingering on her lips, and hearing the joyous greetings of the servants and Mammy Liza's glad welcome as she folded her to her heart. From this dream of bliss she was awakened by a burning kiss pressed on her lips, and a strong arm encircling her. Gazing around and taking in the whole situation, she sprang from her seat, her eyes flashing with rage and scorn, her face flushed to the roots of her hair, her voice shaken with excitement, and every nerve trembling with angry emotion.*
>
> *"How dare you do such a thing! Don't you know if my father were here he would crush you to the earth?"*
>
> *"Not so fast, my lovely tigress," said Bastine, "your father knew what he was doing when he placed you in my charge."* (103–4)

This last sentence, while not literally true as far as the story is concerned, certainly is true metaphorically if we consider the "father" in question to be the white patriarchy that governs the disposal of slave women in the U.S. context. For Iola now *is* a slave woman, practically speaking, and Bastine's behavior toward her in this scene indicates the reconfiguration of her relation to the public and private realms that is wrought through the disclosure of that fact. Heretofore in the discourse of Iola's life, her identity as a Negro had been almost completely secret—unknown even to her—a perversely private affair. With the revelation of that identity—its being made public, as it were—comes Iola's inscription into a literal economy in which her person becomes someone else's private concern; that is to say, she effectively becomes the private property of any white man who conceives an interest in her, and the erotic relation that might develop between her and such a man (symbolized in the case of Bastine by the kiss that he forces on her) becomes the expression of that new disposition and the sign of the black woman's privatized status.[9]

This private-property status need not be literalized in slavery in order to be socially significant; indeed, it continues to be implicated in many forms of the white male/black female relation long after the signing of the Emancipation Proclamation. Because the sudden discovery of her African heritage provides for her particularly dramatic transition to a privatized status, the light-skinned Negro woman is consistently used in various representational contexts to illustrate the social dimensions of such privatization. For instance, in the 1949 movie *Pinky*, directed by Elia Kazan (Twentieth Century-Fox), the light-skinned title character, who has returned to her segregated small southern hometown after passing for some years as a white woman in Boston, is warned by two white men who drive by her in a car that she should not be out walking in the "nigger section" of town. When she informs them that she is walking there because she lives there, they realize that she must be a Negro and thus fair game to be sexually accosted, which they immediately proceed to do; one of them

Pinky (Jeanne Crain) returns to her hometown neighborhood. (*Pinky,* dir. Elia Kazan. Twentieth Century-Fox, 1949). Photo courtesy of Photofest.

nearly succeeds in kissing her before she is able to break away and escape to her grandmother's house.[10]

Both Iola's and Pinky's experiences illustrate the degree to which sexual exploitation of black women by white men in the United States can be characterized as the man's merely exercising his rights with respect to his own private concern, represented in the person of the woman, whose availability for sexual use—which is effectively identical with her racial affiliation—is a matter of public knowledge. This arrangement, while it may cause any amount of discomfort in certain individual citizens, does not, I daresay, produce among social conservatives the great degree of anxiety that we usually consider to be engendered by *miscegenation*; but then, I would not characterize this type of relation as miscegenational for the purposes of my discussion here.

In the two scenarios I have just considered, the disclosure of the women's secret (their true racial identity) immediately alters their relation to the realm of the private such that they become objects in someone else's private domain—specifically, the white man's—and not active subjects who can themselves lay claim to and govern their *own* private domains. Thus the relation between the white man and the black woman that obtains in these narratives presents no threat at all to the subjective power of the white patriarch—indeed it solidifies his subjectivity precisely because it emphasizes the degree to which he is master over his own private realm, king in his own castle, while simultaneously voiding the black woman's subjectivity by depriving her of a private realm over which she can hold sovereign sway.[11] *Miscegenation*, as I want narrowly to define it, denotes sexual relations between two people who, while they are of

Pinky (Jeanne Crain) is comforted by her grandmother (Ethel Waters). (*Pinky,* dir. Elia Kazan. Twentieth Century-Fox, 1949). Photo courtesy of Photofest.

different racial identifications, are nonetheless equal subjects to the extent that they agree to behave as though each has command of a private realm that he or she has consented to "wed" with the other's in a common interest—the "marriage relations" of which Dr. Gresham speaks to Iola (231). My contention, clearly, is that social subjectivity depends upon a person's having control over a body of interests that all concerned parties agree are *private* to that person. The problem, from the perspective of white patriarchal claims, is that such a recognition with respect to certain historically oppressed populations necessarily compromises the white patriarch's own subjective power.[12] Thus miscegenation, insofar as it implies the reconceptualization of a nonwhite individual not as privatized object but as private subject (who would then, by definition, be entitled to hold private property), must represent a profound threat to the political status quo, and consequently a source of severe anxiety throughout "official" culture. Eva Saks puts it this way in her analysis of miscegenation case law in the United States:

> *Miscegenation, which threatened the existing distribution of property and of blood (law's title to race), was therefore a crime by people against property. . . . Interracial sex and marriage had the potential to threaten the distribution of property, and their legal prohibition was an important step in consolidating social and economic boundaries. (49–50)*[13]

Which brings us back to Iola Leroy's assertion regarding her racial identity: "I see no necessity for proclaiming [it] on the house-top. Yet I am resolved that nothing shall tempt me to deny it." It is worth remembering that Iola makes this assertion in the context of her search for gainful employment—for her own private income, which, as we have seen, is precisely what is at stake in the struggle to manage interracial sexual relations. What impresses me most strongly every time I read this passage, however, is the degree to which it sounds like a post-Stonewall assertion about the "private" nature of gay or lesbian identification. Indeed, it seems to me that if we analytically exploit this associative link between the political significances of minority racial and sexual identities—keeping in mind the fundamentally *economic* character of the concerns we have already considered—we may discover that antimiscegenation sentiment and homophobia (or at any rate, institutionalized versions of them prevalent in the United States) derive their impetus largely from a common organizing principle: the sanctity of the private realm as a means for controlling the flow of economic capital.

Homosexual Identity as Foreign Threat

In order to elucidate the foregoing proposition—that institutionalized antimiscegenation sentiment and homophobia are largely rooted in fundamental economic concerns—we may first want to consider some of the specific cultural effects of one of these "official" anxieties. We can conveniently accomplish this by recurring to what has served as the central figure in our inquiry—namely, the kiss. I have already discussed the significance of the kiss in the narrative of the standard heterosexual relation—the teleological function whereby the kiss retroactively invests the heterosexual relation with a fundamentally erotic character, confers upon that character the status of open secret, and founds a realm of personal privacy in terms of which the heterosexual relation derives its social meaning. I have also postulated the rather different significance of the kiss in representations of a certain type of mixed-race relationship, where, rather than implicating a realm of personal privacy, the kiss expresses a relation of private property wherein the white man's sovereignty over his private dominion is solidified at the expense of the black woman's control over her own private realm. Now the question before us is, What does the kiss signify in a same-sex instantiation?

It is evident, I think, that the same-sex kiss *can* serve a function similar to that of the kiss in the narrative of the standard heterosexual relation: that is to say that it makes manifest the erotic character of a relationship previously presenting as nonerotic. If, in the United States, one sees two men or two women kiss—on the lips, in particular—one instantly recasts what one had previously known about that relationship in specifically erotic terms. In this sense, the function of the kiss does not really differ here from its role in the standard heterosexual narrative. What *is* different, though, about the same-sex kiss versus its counterpart in the heterosexual narrative is that the former potentially functions to reveal a secret not only about the character of the *relationship* between the persons who kiss but also about those persons themselves. In other words, owing precisely to the culturally predominant presumption that everyone is heterosexual unless proven otherwise, the same-sex kiss speaks to *identity* in a much more highly charged way than does a kiss between a woman and a man, and in this respect it rather resembles the signal kiss in the narrative of racial secrecy and its revelation, discussed above.

Given this potential of the same-sex kiss to bespeak a homosexual identity for the persons who engage in it—and the threat to social status that such an identity generally constitutes—it is not surprising that extensive cultural safeguards have been constructed to short-circuit that potential in the contexts where such a kiss is likely to occur. The extreme scarcity of such contexts itself attests to the degree of social danger that is generally identified in the same-sex kiss; analysis of how that danger is managed in one of those few cultural sites will further illuminate precisely the terms in which it is generally experienced, and thus the specific character of its social significance.

Earvin "Magic" Johnson and Isiah Thomas, during the 1988 NBA finals. Photo: Andrew D. Bernstein/NBA Photos.

A prime example for consideration here is the masculine realm of professional sports, regarding which Brian Pronger has claimed that "[a] homoerotic text can be gleaned from [its] common discourse."[14] In partial support of this statement, Pronger presents a photograph of the now-famous scene in which professional basketball players Isiah Thomas and Earvin "Magic" Johnson kiss before a tip-off during the 1988 NBA finals. At the present juncture, after Magic Johnson's public announcement of his HIV-seropositivity in 1991, it is impossible not to consider this scene as a constitutive factor in the popular problematization of his sexual identity—the widespread, albeit fairly tacit, recognition that that identity may implicate homosexual activity, despite Johnson's continued insistence that he has had sexual encounters exclusively with women. I would argue that prior to that announcement, however, the kiss between the two players was never considered to have a properly *homosexual* import, or to indicate that Thomas and Johnson were themselves gay. On the contrary, the extensive cultural sanctioning of professional sport's profoundly homosocial character actually sublimates to a conventional hypermasculine significance whatever homoerotically inflected behavior takes place in that context (an extremely interesting camp effect). Consequently, individual players are themselves immunized against being homosexually identified, and the threatening effects of such identification are concomitantly displaced to (and defused in) the abstracted professional-sports "discourse" in which Pronger locates the "homoerotic text" to which he refers. (This fact may even make redundant the disclaimer that appears on the copyright page of Pronger's book: "The presence of the image or name of any person in this book does not necessarily imply that they are homosexual.")

A similar strategy of displacement is in evidence in a 1989 story in the *New York Times* about Darryl Strawberry, then a New York Mets outfielder. Printed in tandem with a photograph of Strawberry kissing teammate Keith Hernandez on the cheek, the story, by George Vecsey, asked, "Was Darryl Strawberry warming up for an exodus to Los Angeles by planting a show-biz smooch on Keith Hernandez's cheek?" It then continued with some cultural explication: "This kind of behavior goes over very well on the Left Coast, where Strawberry hopes to perform in 1991."[15] In this example, the homoerotic potential of the kiss is rendered manageable by, first, framing it not as sexual but as characteristic of a particular professional culture—that is, "show-biz"; and, second, definitively locating that culture in some other place, away from *here*, wherever *here* may happen to be.

Darryl Strawberry and Keith Hernandez, 1989. Photo: AP/Wide World Photos.

Such identification of the homoerotic as a literally foreign characteristic was recapitulated in a June 1990 installment of the sports comic *Tank McNamara,* by Jeff Millar and Bill Hinds. In the strip, which consists of one long panel, two patrons at a bar are watching a sports match on television and exclaiming incredulously about the behavior of the men on the field: "They're *kissing* each other." The bartender responds, "Billions of people are watching the World Cup. Don't you guys want to be cosmopolitan?" The invocation of cosmopolitanism, along with the reference to soccer—that most alien of sports in the U.S. context—neatly implicates foreignness so as to manage the potential homoeroticism of the players' kiss in two divergent and yet complementary ways. On the one hand, these aspects of the bartender's remarks—like Vecsey's discussion of the Darryl

Strawberry incident—suggest that that homoeroticism need not be at all threatening, precisely because it is characteristic of a foreign people who are not at all "like us." On the other hand, to the degree that he seeks through his commentary to nudge his customers out of their resistance to foreign sports custom, the bartender may be seen as trying to cast the soccer players' kiss in terms that will make it intelligible to the bar patrons—as implicitly suggesting the kiss's comparability to conventional instances of masculine homosocial affection in U.S. professional sports and thereby rendering the kiss similarly void of recognized homoerotic import.

This engineered comparability of the soccer players' kiss and characteristic practices from other cultural contexts suggests the degree to which such practices—for all their publicness in the contexts under consideration—nonetheless derive their significance from a highly pervasive and influential logic of privacy. For, indeed, one of the defining characteristics—I am tempted to call it one of the chief beauties—of the private domain in capitalist society is precisely that anything in it can be rendered equivalent to, and thus exchangeable for, any other private interest. This is not to suggest that the social *meanings* of, say, a kiss between two persons of different sexes and a kiss between two persons of the same sex are identical; it *is* to suggest, however, that, in the cultural as in the market economy, comparable social *values* can be extracted from such otherwise disparately signifying phenomena. According to this logic—which we must, I think, identify as a fundamentally conservative one—not only do homosexual relationships begin to look a lot like heterosexual ones, with the same claims to protection as private interests,[16] but they also, metaphorically, represent the possible encroachment of "foreign" interests on the conventional domestic economy. Thus homosexual panic—the fear of a sort of "domino effect" by which homosexual subjects inexorably recruit to our cause ever increasing numbers of

TANK McNAMARA® **by Jeff Millar & Bill Hinds**

Tank McNamara. Copyright © 1990 Millar/Hinds. Dist. by Universal Press Syndicate.

heretofore "innocent" parties—resembles anxiety over the encroachment of alien claims on the domestic sphere. The extent to which such anxiety founds officially sanctioned homophobic activity in U.S. culture can be discerned through consideration of one particularly notorious recent legal case.

Until 1983, Sharon Kowalski and Karen Thompson maintained a closeted lesbian relationship in St. Cloud, Minnesota, having made no legal provisions by which to protect their attachment. In 1983, Kowalski was in a car accident that left her seriously disabled, unable either to speak or to walk. When Kowalski's father, after some elapse of time, obtained sole guardianship of his daughter, he moved her to a nursing home in rural Minnesota and prohibited Thompson from visiting her. From 1985 until 1989, Thompson fought in the courts for the right to see Kowalski, eventually winning a court order granting her visiting privileges, which she enjoyed for the next two years. Kowalski's father, citing poor health, resigned as his daughter's guardian in May 1990, but when Thompson applied to be appointed guardian her request was denied by State District Court Judge Robert Campbell, who chastised Thompson for violating Kowalski's privacy by informing Kowalski's parents and a concerned gay and lesbian constituency of Kowalski's lesbian involvement in the first place.[17] In December 1991, the Minnesota Court of Appeals reversed Campbell's finding and granted guardianship to Thompson.[18] By that time, however, Campbell's decision had already emphatically underscored the point that the Supreme Court dramatically registered in its 1986 *Bowers v. Hardwick* decision—that the condition of privacy and the personal protections it is thought to imply do not extend to lesbians and gay men, however much activists committed to working through standard legal channels might insist otherwise.[19] For what the state clearly was interested in maintaining as inviolate in the Kowalski case was not the "private" character of the homosexual relation (the fundamental terms of which it saw as having already been violated in the process of being rendered recognizable) but, rather, the private interest of the heterosexually constituted nuclear family against which the claims of the lesbian couple represented a serious foreign threat. That threat might at first glance appear to consist merely in the alienation of affective ties among the blood relations comprised in the nuclear family, but this is only because we have been carefully trained to recognize as mere affective interest what is really at stake in the constitution of the family unit: distribution of property and other material benefits through, among other mechanisms, legal inheritance.

At this point, then, we can clearly discern the common sociopolitical significance of homosexual relations, on the one hand, and the mixed-race ones discussed above, on the other. For the fracturing of the heterosexually-oriented boundaries that have traditionally defined the family structure portends as profound a disruption in the orderly distribution of material wealth in our era as did the subversion of clearly traceable "blood lines" by miscegenation in the nineteenth century. What this means, for those of us who are interested in the construction of cultural mechanisms by which to understand and combat the social and political forces that keep lesbians and gay men in check, is that the history of racial politics in this country, beyond merely providing us with a "model" for activism—as it has long been acknowledged to do—may actually prove to be the context in which the very terms of our predicament are founded. If so, then our continual recurrence to that history must constitute not an effectively "academic" exercise, in which we assert problematic parallels between highly specific sociopolitical phenomena, but rather a sort of archaeological engagement, through which we discover a critical logic that might govern and render effective the strategies of resistance that, one way or another, we necessarily will undertake.

1990–1994

Notes

1. Bernard Champigneulle, *Rodin,* trans. and adapt. J. Maxwell Brownjohn (New York: Abrams, 1967) 157.

2. Albert E. Elsen, "When the Sculptures Were White," exhibition catalog for *Rodin Rediscovered,* ed. Elsen (Washington, D.C.: National Gallery of Art; Boston: Little, Brown/New York Graphic Society, 1981) 136–37.

3. Sidney Geist, *Brancusi: A Study of the Sculpture* (New York: Grossman, 1968) 142.

4. Frank Whitford, *Klimt,* World of Art (London and New York: Thames and Hudson, 1990) 118.

5. D. A. Miller, "Secret Subjects, Open Secrets," *The Novel and the Police* (Berkeley: University of California Press, 1988) 206.

6. Frances Ellen Watkins Harper, *Iola Leroy; or, Shadows Uplifted* (1892), intro. Hazel V. Carby, Black Women Writers, series ed. Deborah E. McDowell (Boston: Beacon, 1987) 230–31 for the quoted passage.

7. For a comprehensive analysis of miscegenation case law from the early nineteenth century through the late twentieth, see Eva Saks, "Representing Miscegenation Law," *Raritan* 8.2 (Fall 1988): 39–69.

8. See, for instance, Carole Pateman, "Feminist Critiques of the Public/Private Dichotomy," in *The Disorder of Women: Democracy, Feminism and Political Theory* (Stanford: Stanford University Press, 1989) 118–40.

9. The conceptual linkage between two types of privacy that I am implicitly exploiting here—between the conditions of secrecy and social discretion, on the one hand, and of proprietorship, on the other—can paradoxically best be discerned in the argument put forth in a 1981 *Harvard Law Review* article that asserts the fundamental *distinction* between the two in U.S. legal history.

In tracing the development of the legal right to personal privacy—conceived as disjunct from the right to own private property—the authors of this piece derive that right from, among other sources, nineteenth-century case law against eavesdropping, in which it was determined that "no man has a right . . . to pry into your secrecy in your own house" ("The Right to Privacy in Nineteenth-Century America," *Harvard Law Review* 94.8 [June 1981]: 1896). They thus conceive of personal privacy predominantly as a function of the effective private-property context in which it is recognized (the implicitly operative legal maxim "a man's house is his castle" connoting possession by occupation, if not by title), despite the putative independence of the two concepts. For more on the various legal conceptions of privacy—and further evidence of the degree to which the relation between personal privacy and private property is purposefully and suspiciously obscured in conventional legal thought—see Vincent J. Samar, *The Right to Privacy: Gays, Lesbians, and the Constitution* (Philadelphia: Temple University Press, 1991) especially chapter 1, "The Objects of Legal Privacy" (13–49); and Samuel D. Warren and Louis D. Brandeis, "The Right to Privacy," *Harvard Law Review* 4.5 (15 December 1890): 193–220.

However strenuously the personal privacy–private property link might be denied by legal commentators, it nonetheless seems to enjoy a high degree of popular recognition. For instance, the narrated text in a recently aired radio advertisement for a Boston-area reproductive health clinic indicates that "Repro Associates is a private practice devoted to reproductive health—because in some matters, it's privacy that counts," thus powerfully identifying the private status of the corporation with the private character of its clientele's concerns (advertisement broadcast during the program *Matty in the Morning,* WXKS, Medford, Mass., 13 January 1993).

10. I am grateful to Cindy Patton for directing my attention to this scene.

11. Thus property relations help constitute not only personal privacy (as I explain in note 9) but also *private* (i.e., domestic) *life.* Of course, the theorization of that constitutive function, which is by no means complete, has a history reaching at least as far back as Friedrich Engels (see *The Origin of the Family, Private Property, and the State* [1884; New York: International Publishers, 1942]).

The ramifications of the particular type of interracial, intergender relation that I am describing here are compellingly addressed by Patricia J. Williams. See her essay "On Being the Object of Property," in *The Alchemy of Race and Rights* (Cambridge: Harvard University Press, 1991) 216–36.

12. The centrality of the white subject's interest in the phenomenon of miscegenation is indicated in the dictionary definition of the term, which characterizes it as denoting especially "marriage between white and nonwhite persons." See "miscegenation," in *The American Heritage Dictionary of the English Language,* ed. William Morris (Boston: Houghton Mifflin, 1973).

13. The point that Saks makes is rendered particularly explicit in another novel from the same period as *Iola Leroy.* In Charles Chesnutt's *The Marrow of Tradition,* a white character's profound hatred of her mixed-race half sister is based precisely on her fear that this sister will lay claim to a portion of their dead father's estate. When the white sister confesses her anxiety to her husband, he reassures her in terms that strongly resonate with the point I make above—that the black woman's relative powerlessness as a private subject is a function of her effective status as private property: ". . . [W]ho was she," he demands, "to have inherited the estate of your ancestors, of which, a few years before, she would herself have formed a part?" (Charles W. Chesnutt, *The Marrow of Tradition* [1901; New York: Arno Press, 1969] 256). I am indebted to Lee Edelman for suggesting to me the pertinence of Chesnutt's work to my argument in this essay.

14. Brian Pronger, *The Arena of Masculinity: Sports, Homosexuality, and the Meaning of Sex* (New York: St. Martin's, 1990) 191.

15. George Vecsey, "Sports of the Times: Strawberry: One Kiss, One Homer," *New York Times* 5 March 1989: section 8, p. 2.

16. These claims are characteristically invoked by conservative gay activists whose objective is to achieve the extension of "civil rights" to gays and lesbians without calling into question the basis on which those rights are founded in the first place. See, for instance, David LaFontaine and Patrick Ward, "Why our future is in the GOP," *Gay Community News* 18.28 (4–10 February 1991): 5.

17. For a concise overview of the case, see Nan D. Hunter, "Sexual Dissent and the Family" *The Nation* 253.11 (7 October 1991): 406–11.

18. Dawn Schmitz, "Kowalski and Thompson win!" *Gay Community News* 19.23 (22 December 1991–4 January 1992): 1, 6, 12.

19. *Bowers, Attorney General of Georgia v. Hardwick et al.,* 478 U.S. 186–220 (1986).

2 "The Subversive Edge"

Paris Is Burning, Social Critique, and the Limits of Subjective Agency

Drag Presentation and Public Effect

To judge from popular-press reviews that greeted its release, Jennie Livingston's film *Paris Is Burning* (Off-White Productions, 1991) has left a significant number of its viewers pleasantly surprised. What surprises them is not only what was widely registered as Livingston's intrepidness in venturing among the black and Latino habitués of Harlem's drag-ball scene, which the film portrays,[1] but also—and more significantly—the activities of the film's subjects themselves, particularly their precise replication (in the context of the balls' regimented competitions) of the styles and behaviors of a range of social types recognizable from daily life, from mass-media projections, or from both. John Howell, commenting in 1989 on rough-cut footage from what was then Livingston's work-in-progress, gives a fairly typical account of contestants' achievement of such "Realness," as it is called in the ball context:

In costume and poise, these artificial Yalies and businessmen would be utterly indistinguishable from the "real thing" on the campus or in the office. Similarly, any general would salute troops who paraded with the spit-and-polish panache of the voguers who impersonate marines. Every detail is duplicated to the minutest degree, from body language to personality, from clothing to accessories (briefcases, American Express cards, airplane tickets, and Wall Street Journals *for the businessmen, letter sweaters and textbooks for the students).*[2]

If the "perfection" with which ball contestants assume the aspects "of our society's most normative roles" occasions wonder among critical observers (Howell 11), these observers' pleasure in being thus surprised derives from the significance with which they invest those precise replications, which is of a particular kind. Writing in *Mother Jones*, reviewer Jim Farber remarked that

[f]ootage of [the] contests takes up a good part of the movie, along with scenes of the voguers at home, constructing their identities. The personality overhauls give the balls a subversive edge, stressing the sly mutability of identity.[3]

Key here is the *subversiveness* that Farber discerns in the stylizations of the "voguers"—notable instances of which, it must be emphasized, entail "male-to-female" drag performance—for it seems clear that this subversiveness constitutes not only the "angle that first attracted Livingston" to ball culture (Farber) but also the ostensible primary object of interest offered by that culture to Farber himself, and thus, by extension, to the social liberals comprised in his readership. If, as I am suggesting, this subversiveness pleases them, it is because it seems to characterize as politically acceptable a phenomenon whose progressiveness must be questionable at first glance because of both the distinctly *cultural*—not to say *frivolous*—mode of its intervention (as opposed to, say, a properly *economic* one), which renders it unorthodox as a political undertaking in any event, and the particularly conflicted significance of such cultural intervention in the contemporary, postmodern context.

It is easy enough to identify the constituent factors in the reputed subversiveness of ball culture. Jim Farber's own formulation makes it quite clear that it is the demonstration of the "mutability of identity"—effected in particular through ball contestants' achievement of Realness—that provides the requisite "edge" to the culture's sociopolitical significance. According to John Howell, that demonstration inevitably raises the questions: "[W]hat is authentic in social roles? Who does our culture reward and who does it exclude, and how different are they? What is male, what is female? Can our chromosomal hard-wiring be reprogrammed?" Howell's identification of these as "bottom-line questions" implies that the mere posing of them is a radical political act; and since, according to Howell, it is "voguing" itself that thus "leads us to deep issues" (11), ball practice emerges, in his rendering, as the clear agent of subversive critique.

But, of course, however critically efficacious it may be, Realness styling itself appears as the effect of a motivated regimen undertaken by specific identifiable agents, namely, the "voguers" who, in Farber's terms, achieve "personality overhauls" by actively "constructing their identities." These formulations manifest a curious conflation. By way of indicating the intentionality of their efforts to make themselves over as recognizable types—to "overhaul" their attitudes and appearances, as they indisputably do—Farber concomitantly suggests that the ball contestants enact an equally voluntaristic transformation in their very *selves*, figured here as their "personalities" and "identities." The positing of such an accomplishment is potentially appealing for at least two closely related reasons: (1) it imputes to denizens of the ball milieu an expanded agency whereby they seem able to alter apparently fundamental elements of social experience; and (2) it thus recuperates those same personages as active producers not only of political critique but of significant social-structural change.

Thus the attractiveness of this scenario is easy to understand. After all, a (if not *the*) primary challenge of contemporary culture is the achievement of some degree of resistant political agency that isn't immediately undercut by any of the various infrastructural mechanisms through which it is registered and disseminated; and for such agency to be achieved by persons who are profoundly socially and politically marginalized as poor, gay blacks and Latinos/as would be particularly heartening. Whatever the desirability of that achievement, though, it is by no means clear that it actually occurs in the drag-ball context—that, in other words, the effective subjectivity exercised by the ball queens in the overhauling of their appearances constitutes such sociopolitical agency as would be entailed in the "constructing of their identities." For this latter agency implies a capacity not only to style one's aspect but to exercise some control over the conditions of its general reception. However much they might enjoy such a capacity in the ballroom, the subjects of *Paris Is Burning* were definitively shown to lack it beyond the ball context when they attempted to redefine the terms of the film's success.

As Jesse Green reported in an update on the ball scene published in the *New York Times* two years after the release of *Paris Is Burning*, all but two of the queens featured in the film filed legal claims against Jennie Livingston once the movie started to turn a profit:

The largest claim came from Paris DuPree, who sought $40 million for unauthorized and fraudulent use of services. Though Paris is never named on camera and appears for less than three of the movie's 76 minutes, Paris's 1986 ball provided the title for the film and is extensively featured in it. But like all of the others, Paris had signed a release, and the matter was dropped.[4]

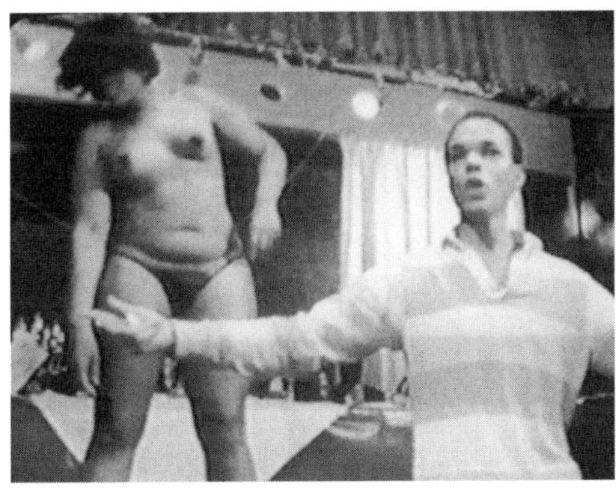

Paris DuPree presides over the "Luscious Body" competition during the ball featured in *Paris Is Burning* (dir. Jennie Livingston, Off-White Productions, 1991).

On its surface, and in Green's flatly declarative rendering, the dismissal of DuPree's complaint seems a thoroughly straightforward legal-procedural affair: DuPree had signed a release; the matter was dropped. The powerful subjective agency that DuPree purportedly enjoys in the ballroom is thus checked, in the juridical realm, by precisely such technical factors as seem to distinguish the juridical as a fundamentally different sphere from that constituted by the balls. I would argue, however, that the very recognition of such factors is necessitated by the degree to which the juridical context and the drag-ball milieu represent different aspects of the *same* realm, in either of which the queens featured in *Paris Is Burning* might thus achieve an agency that is socially significant and politically potent.

For all the evident differences between courtroom and ballroom—not the least of which is that the former constitutes an element of state administration while the latter most emphatically does not—both of them nonetheless partake in what is so fundamental an attribute of the *public* as to inform all the disparate formulations of that sphere.[5] In short, both sites are characterized by such activities of social *self-presentation* as are central not merely to the perpetuation of state authority and to the constitution of subjective identity but also to the exercise of community citizenship, the symbolism of market exchange, and the workings of mass media, all of which have been theorized as constituting the public sphere (see Robbins xiii–xx). The

conceptualization of both the juridical arena and the drag-ball site as instantiations of the public suggests that the subjects of Livingston's film might substantively intervene in the one just as easily as in the other. If they fail in this undertaking, as they evidently do, there are compelling reasons *why*—reasons whose significance is actually thematized in the process whereby *Paris Is Burning* effects its own sociocultural intervention.

Performativity and Subjective Agency

Before we can successfully theorize the constraint on their subjectivity that the ball queens suffer, we must first determine the specific character of the agency that they enjoy in the ball context. I have already indicated that that agency cannot be understood as the queens' ability to "construct their personalities" in the active and voluntaristic manner that Jim Farber suggests. Indeed, Farber's postulation resembles nothing so much as the misapprehensions of "gender performativity" that have largely characterized theoretical discussion since the publication of Judith Butler's highly influential *Gender Trouble* in 1990.[6] Butler herself has recognized the degree to which her theory has been misunderstood, identifying as the primary misapprehension the idea

> *that gender is a choice, or that gender is a role, or that gender is a construction that one puts on, as one puts on clothes in the morning, that there is a "one" who is prior to this gender, a one who goes to the wardrobe of gender and decides with deliberation which gender it will be today.*[7]

This misapprehension is based largely, as Butler makes clear, on the limited understanding of "performativity" as denoting specifically and merely a mode of *theatrical* production. Much more centrally at work in Butler's theory is the concept of performativity as a mode of *discursive* production. While the structural relation between these two types of performativity might certainly be interrogated to valuable theoretical effect, as in Eve Kosofsky Sedgwick's recent work on the significance of shame to "queer performativity,"[8] there is little to be gained from the far more common elision of performativity's discursive significance and the concomitant critical emphasis on its theatrical import, a mistake that Butler insightfully traces to "the political needs of a growing queer movement in which the publicization of theatrical agency has become quite central" ("Critically Queer" 21).

Indeed, what is so important about Butler's work is that it profoundly problematizes the very notion of subjective agency, getting at that critique through an interrogation of gender as an instance of specifically *discursive* rather than *theatrical* performativity. Butler—as does Sedgwick, practically in tandem with her—usefully traces the genealogy of the theory of discursive performativity to its effective protoconcept: performativity (all too easily apprehended as specifically *linguistic*) in the sense first elaborated by J. L. Austin in *How to Do Things with Words*.[9] Invoking (and thereby establishing as paradigmatic) the example of the heterosexual wedding vow—"I do [sc. take this woman to be my lawful wedded wife]" (5 and passim)—Austin characterized as "performative" those utterances the issuing of which "is the performing of an action" (6).

As Butler is at pains to make clear, however, the force of the performative derives not from the subject who utters it but rather from a regulatory matrix constituted by the legacy of discursive acts into which it emerges and which it effectively "cites" ("Critically Queer" 17–18). It is the derivation of its force from within this legacy that renders the performative properly *discursive* and that, further, unsettles the notion of individual agential subjectivity on which depend both the conventional understanding of gender identity as an essential attribute and mistaken notions of its *theatrically* performative quality. In contradistinction to these, Butler sees gender as neither constituting nor indicating the existence of a subjective "core" or "self" but, rather, as performatively established within a discursive matrix the elements of which are not—or at least not *primarily*—linguistic but gestural or behavioral:

> *[A]cts, gestures, and desire produce the effect of an internal core or substance. . . . [They] are* performative *in the sense that the essence or identity that they otherwise purport to express are* fabrications *manufactured and sustained through corporeal signs and other discursive means. . . . [A]cts and gestures, articulated and enacted desires create the illusion of an interior and organizing gender core. . . . (*Gender Trouble *136, emphasis in original)*

This illusion, Butler further asserts, serves a disciplinary function; it

> *is discursively maintained for the purposes of the regulation of sexuality within the obligatory frame of reproductive heterosexuality. If the "cause" of desire, gesture, and act can be localized within the "self" of the actor, then the political regulations and disciplinary practices which produce that ostensibly coherent gender are effectively displaced from view. The displacement of a political and discursive origin of gender identity onto a psychological "core" precludes an analysis of the political constitution of the gendered subject and its fabricated notions about the ineffable interiority of its sex or of its true identity. (*Gender Trouble *136)*

Thus Butler's deconstruction of gender (which is coextensive, according to her analysis, with identity as such)—her exposition of it as discursively performative—renders untenable any conception of an agential subject that would *theatrically* perform, or voluntaristically "construct," an identity through the manipulation of various effects taken to signify gender (for instance) in conventional contexts. With the impossibility of effective "personality overhauls" thus demonstrated, the stylizations of the drag balls' Realness queens lose the specific "subversive edge" that Jim Farber has imputed to them.

This is not to say, however, that Realness posing—or any instance of more "conventional" cross-gender drag, for that matter—serves no critical function at all. It is merely to say (again, following Butler) that that critical function *does not* consist in drag's serving as "a sign of the essential plasticity of gender" ("Critically Queer" 25). Rather, according to Butler's explication, drag's real "edge" lies in the fact that it "exposes or allegorizes the mundane psychic and performative practices by which heterosexualized genders form themselves through the renunciation of the *possibility* of homosexuality. . . . Drag thus allegorizes *heterosexual melancholy*" ("Critically Queer" 25, emphasis in original), which Butler identifies, in the sections of *Gender Trouble* that engage psychoanalytic theory, as the initiatory force behind the performative construction of normative genders (57–72).

The crucial difference, then, between this conception of drag's "subversiveness" and the one suggested in accounts such as Farber's has to do with the place of subjective agency. The latter conception posits an individual subjective agency that it conceives as capable of voluntaristically fashioning its own "self"—a conception that is problematic insofar as any effective "self" has already been performatively constituted within a regulatory discursive matrix that both precedes and continually conditions it. In other words, the discursive performativity through which "selves" are brought into being by its very nature *precludes* the participation of such selves as productive subjects within that operation.

On the other hand, the expositional-allegorical function in which Butler locates drag's critical force depends on individual agency not to "construct" its own self—to intervene in and govern the process of discursive performativity—but rather to enact a *theatrical performance* whereby the mechanism through which gender is

constituted is effectively exposed. It is precisely in the terms of this difference—which we might think of as the capacity for critical *deconstruction* versus the ability to effect substantive social *reconstruction*—that we can also characterize the distinction between ballroom and courtroom, the two aspects of the public realm that figure so centrally in the drama of *Paris Is Burning* and that the drag queens presented in the film attempt to negotiate with radically disparate results.

The Imaginary Real

We can achieve a sense of the crucial difference between the ballroom and courtroom sites by referring to Judith Butler's own examination of *Paris Is Burning*, which usefully refines the proposition that there is no place for subjective agency in the performative constitution of an individual "self." Focusing on various ball participants' (and especially Venus Xtravaganza's) expert citation of gestures comprised in the constitution of normative class, race, and gender identities, Butler suggests that this voluntaristic performance actually *does* result in the production of an identifiable subject—a suggestion that implies not the negation of prior claims as to the impossibility of such a production but, rather, the peculiar character of the subject that emerges in Realness posturing.

Butler asserts that "[i]n the drag ball productions of realness, we witness and produce the phantasmatic constitution of a subject, a subject who repeats and mimes the legitimating norms by which it itself has been degraded."[10] The subject that emerges through enactments of drag-ball Realness is *phantasmatically* constituted, but this in and of itself does not distinguish it from the normative subjects that it recalls. For they, too—and this is what Realness posturing exposes, according to Butler—are "phantasmatically instituted and sustained"

("Gender Is Burning" 130). Rather, the critical difference between normative subjects and those produced in the enactment of Realness is that the former are discursively constituted as recognizable within the governing social structure and thus are legitimated in a way that the latter are not. In other words, normative subjectivities comprise "sanctioned fantasies, sanctioned imaginaries, [which] are insidiously elevated as the parameters of realness" ("Gender Is Burning" 130). Thus, "Realness" is what is recognized in the ball context but not beyond it; "realness" characterizes subjectivities recognized in the larger social field and might usefully be understood in Lacanian terms as corresponding not to the homonymous order of the Real but rather to the realm of the *symbolic*.[11]

Venus Xtravaganza, seated on a friend's lap, in a scene from *Paris Is Burning* (dir. Jennie Livingston, Off-White Productions, 1991). Photo: Everett Collection.

The Lacanian conception is useful in that it can help us to understand the relation between the sanctioning of social norms and the specific public function of the juridical realm, as opposed to that of drag-ball practice. As a conditioning factor in the constitution of the subject, the Lacanian register of the *symbolic* derives its significance specifically in relation to the order of the *imaginary*. Figured in terms of discursive logic, the imaginary denotes the experiential mode in which a speaking subject conceives of itself as fully present in, represented by, and in control of the discourse that it produces. The symbolic, on the other hand, comprises the mode in which that subject recognizes the fundamental disjuncture between itself and its discursive representation—the fact that, as Antony Easthope neatly puts it, "the 'I' as represented in discourse . . . is always sliding away from the 'I' doing the speaking"—and, relatedly, that the significance of the discourse that it produces is governed by relations beyond its control.[12]

The primary import of the subject's interpellation in the symbolic order is that the subject can never fully (re)present itself in its own enunciations, can never completely "speak (for) itself." This truth does not preclude the subject's becoming adequately functional, but it does indicate the limits to discursive self-effectivity that the subject must negotiate in order to achieve its functionality. In the Lacanian conception, that negotiation consists in the subject's constant oscillation between the equally necessary states of the symbolic and the imaginary. As we have noted, however, the discursive field that constitutes the symbolic order is not subject to voluntaristic manipulation by the individual subjects implicated within it. Consequently, successful "oscillation" *into* the symbolic always entails, as well, the subject's *accommodation* to it. In other words, when Realness queens exit the ball milieu, which constitutes a type of imaginary realm, they must—to all appearances, at least—conform to the norms of the larger social context that effectively constitutes the symbolic order. To be perceived as failing or refusing thus to conform can result in tragic consequences for any given individual. Butler cites a specific, relatively contingent instance of such tragedy that is referenced in *Paris Is Burning*—the eventual murder of Venus Xtravaganza, apparently by a trick who has discovered that she is not a "real" woman at all, in normative terms ("Gender Is Burning" 131). Of greater import for my consideration here, though, is the fact that such disciplinary practice as Venus's murder so brutally instantiated characteristically assumes a rather more systemic manifestation, in which the juridical realm is centrally implicated; for it is this implication that confers upon the juridical apparatus its distinctive public significance.

Precisely to the extent that it represents state administration, as well as other recognized forms of social authority, the courtroom constitutes an aspect of the social-symbolic realm in a way that the drag ballroom—which, for all its similarly public character, embodies no such authority—cannot. Indeed, not only do the instances of social self-presentation manifested in the juridical context constitute such socially sanctioned "fantasies" as are comprised in the symbolic realm but, further, their very manifestation in the arena of official "judgment" dramatically constitutes both that sanctioning and the condemnation of those self-presentations that are not thus legitimated. In other words, juridical activity not only *conforms to* but actually helps to *establish* the terms of legitimacy that condition society as a whole. This is a powerful effect that cannot be said to characterize the drag-ball context, and its absence from that setting founds the inability of the subjects that emerge therein to bring about substantive social-structural change.

This said, it is crucial to emphasize that state apparatuses do not have a monopoly on the establishment and promulgation of normative social modes. Indeed, the importance of cultural productions to these processes has grown apace with the increasing implication of the mass media in contemporary social life. If the cultural practices that characterize the drag-ball context do not partake in the social regulatory function that the juridical apparatus enacts, this is only because they do not represent the same investment of capital—both economic and social-symbolic—as do other types of cultural production, of which Jennie Livingston's film is a primary instance.

Cultural Authorship/Cultural Authority

Given the constraints on their subjectivity that Realness queens clearly suffer, *Paris Is Burning* must be understood not as neutrally "(re)presenting" their effective (and subversive) exercise of sociopolitical agency—their substantive intervention in the very constitution of the symbolic realm—but rather as potentially underwriting the possibility of such exercise. The film's ability to do this is founded in the specific quality of its own public status, which derives largely from its mass-media character, and thus implicates a potentially even farther-ranging social-constitutive function than that enacted in the juridical realm. In its capacity as a highly privileged symbolic apparatus, the film can disseminate the "message" of drag-ball practice to a wide audience beyond the ball context, thus enabling the queens' social intervention, as both Butler and bell hooks have pointed out.[13] At the same time, however—and as Butler and hooks both indicate, as well—the very privilege that Livingston's work enjoys not only potentially augments the effective agency of the drag-ball queens but also works to thwart its realization. This is because the film's *dissemination* of the critique implicit in the queens' activity must always also be a *rearticulation,* insofar as its objective is to render intelligible in the larger social sphere discursive practices that do not partake of its terms in normative modes. It is specifically in this rearticulation that the film's underwriting of the ball queens' subjective agency becomes dubious, since the very mechanism of the film genre—not merely technically but in its contemporary social function—serves the promotion of the *auteur's* subjectivity rather than, and at the expense of, that of the individual(s) understood to be the "subject(s)" of documentary cinema.

In the sections of their works cited above, Butler and hooks provide (not altogether identical) analyses of this phenomenon as it takes place in the cinematic context proper and, in the case of hooks,

Some of the queens featured in *Paris Is Burning* (dir. Jennie Livingston, Off-White Productions, 1991), in a publicity still for the film. Photo: Everett Collection.

in journalistic interviews with Livingston meant to provide both background on the film's production and an account of Livingston's development as a filmmaker. It is worth noting, though, that the journalistic suppression of the queens' subjectivities in favor of Livingston's is a function not only of the potent *auteurism* that conceives the filmmaker, per se, as cultural *author*, but also of a governing discourse that conceives the *documentary* filmmaker as cultural *authority*. This discourse is one in which the review articles by Jim Farber and John Howell extensively participate, thus emblematizing the general process whereby Jennie Livingston's social subjectivity is recognized and legitimated while that of the queens presented in her film is effectively constrained.

As is typical for their genre, both articles assess the overall "quality" of Livingston's film, but they also provide some account of the "subculture" that the film purports to "document." Howell, for instance, undertakes to explain to his readers the signal elements of drag-ball competition:

Appropriately, one of the most important categories is called "Realness," a highly codified and sophisticated classification in which the participant attempts to create a certain "normality." As Livingston explains it, "In Realness, femme queens try to pass for 'real' women, while butch queens compete to duplicate the look of a 'real'—or heterosexual—man." (9)

Farber, for his part, tends more toward critique:

The voguers in Paris Is Burning *often lust after the emptiest possible images of success. Their greatest goal is to become super-rich models—to act out an episode of* Runaway with the Rich and Famous *starring Iman. "I never felt comfortable being poor, or even middle class doesn't suit me," one voguer confides during the film.*

Livingston says that vogueing wasn't always so materialistic. "In the sixties, there were drag balls, but there was lots of individualism and freedom of expression. Then, as the outside world got more yuppie, voguers got into designer labels. It followed the evolution of greed in America."

In each instance, a claim about some key aspect of drag-ball culture—one of its primary organizational principles in the former example, its historical development in the latter—is substantiated by recourse not to actual participants in the culture, whom we might expect to be able to explicate it best, but to Livingston, who has cinematically "documented" it. By thus giving Livingston the final "word" on the phenomena they address, these pieces clearly manifest and reinscribe what I have already referred to as documentary film's *rearticulative* function, but they also indicate the degree to which that function itself grounds the analytical authority enjoyed by the documentary filmmaker within official culture. The extent of that authority is probably best suggested by its conceptualization in terms not of artistic creation but of scientific discipline: consider, for instance, Vincent Canby's declaration that in *Paris Is Burning* Livingston "studies" her subjects "with the curiosity of a compassionate anthropologist."[14]

The degree to which the authority of the documentary filmmaker is thus expanded beyond the strictly cultural-artistic realm into the social-scientific suggests the degree to which the effective agency of her documentary "subjects" is, conversely, diminished in the larger social sphere. For while the impact of *Paris Is Burning* may depend on how successfully it renders ball culture generally recognizable, the intervention thus effected is registered specifically as that of the filmmaker, who is accordingly interpellated as a figure of some social standing, rather than that of the queens on the drag-ball circuit, who clearly are not. As Livingston herself noted some two years after her film's release, "I am now a film maker. . . . And that's something I wasn't before"; at the same time, to quote from Jesse Green's *New York Times* article, in which that self-characterization appears, those presented in *Paris Is Burning* "remain[ed], at best, exactly where they were when filmed" (Green 11).[15] That discrepancy is the effect not so

Filmmaker Jennie Livingston. Photo: Everett Collection.

much of any conscious action by Livingston herself (the faults of her film that Butler and, especially, hooks identify notwithstanding) as of structural constraints on the queens' own subjective agency that attend the limits of the public significance of the drag-ball context—constraints that Livingston could not but exploit once she determined to undertake her documentary project.

Privacy, Property, and Documentary Subjects

We know of the constraint faced by those featured in *Paris Is Burning* when they sought legal rights to profits generated by the film. We also know, from Jesse Green's *New York Times* article, that the grounds for the dismissal of the queens' complaints against Jennie Livingston consisted in their having signed a "release" prior to the film's production. It is worth considering carefully, however, exactly what was "released" by the queens' subscribing to the pertinent documents, and according to what recognized legal principle. Green's account makes it clear that the paperwork covered the queens' provision to the filmmaker of certain "services," one of which would have to have been access to the balls themselves. But of what do the balls consist but the motivated activities of the various persons who participate in them, the exposure of which before the filmmaker's camera might also be seen as a service rendered?

Such publicization of personal activities as is comprised in *Paris Is Burning* is governed by an extensive body of privacy law that it will be useful to consider here. The point of this consideration is not to reassess the legality of the arrangements that Livingston made with her subjects, an undertaking that would be futile as well as presumptuous; rather, it is to make clear the relation between the conventions of documentary film and juridical regulation whereby the former necessitate particular instances of the latter. This demonstration will further

indicate not just the limits of the documentary subjects' agency but the only potential means by which those limits might be overcome in the contemporary sociocultural context.

There are actually three realms of privacy that have been recognized by U.S. courts: Fourth Amendment privacy, comprising limitations on unreasonable search and seizure; constitutional privacy, generally construed as governing marriage relations and reproductive rights; and, what concerns us here, torts privacy, characterized most simply as the "right of the individual to be let alone."[16] Or, perhaps I should say, most *simplistically*, for the phrase above, taken from the 1890 *Harvard Law Review* article that effectively founded torts law privacy, scarcely hints at the range of objects that would eventually be protected under its aegis, the breadth of which must partly fuel the continuing controversy among legal theorists and historians over the very validity of the torts privacy category.

The debate centers on whether the authors of the 1890 article, Samuel Warren and Louis Brandeis, discover legal and factual grounding sufficient to conceive a privacy right distinct from that specified in the Fourth Amendment.[17] Indeed, it is worth noting that some of Warren's and Brandeis's language seems to verge on Fourth Amendment considerations insofar as it manifests a specific concern with the bounded sanctity of habitable realms—in its invocation, for instance, of "the sacred precincts of private and domestic life" (195).

As Jane Gaines has pointed out, however, even this founding article manifests the metonymic shift (which Gaines argues becomes increasingly pronounced throughout the twentieth century) from concern for "sacred precincts," per se, to concern for the *personal quality* of the effects and activities potentially located in and associated with them.[18] For example, in their explicit worry that "what is whispered in the closet shall be proclaimed from the house-tops" (195), Warren and Brandeis betray a concern not for the boundaries of the "closet" themselves but rather over the publication of the intimacies that take place therein. Similarly, their interest in the "sacred precincts" that they invoke has to do specifically with guarding them against "invasion" by agents of publicity, namely "[i]nstantaneous photographs and newspaper enterprise"; and they emphasize that "the law must afford some remedy for the unauthorized circulation of portraits of private persons" (195).

This brief examination of Warren's and Brandeis's text thus makes clear the means by which the mechanically reproduced image—whether still-photographic or cinematic—is conceptualized as an object of privacy, and, further, when it constitutes a cultural commodity, as an object of *intellectual property*. Such an image—which it will be useful to specify as a *visual* image—is only one component, however, in the more complex entity generated through the production, distribution, and exhibition of cinematic film. That entity might be designated as the *personal* image associated with any individual who appears in a given film. Not only would this personal image comprise the activities enacted before Jennie Livingston's camera by the queens featured in her film, it also—like a person's *visual* image—constitutes an object of intellectual property. Since it is in the personal image that we can best discern the interrelation of documentary convention and juridical regulation that conditions the status of the documentary subject, it is worth considering its specific character in some detail.

Jane Gaines offers a viable model for such a consideration in her treatment of the cinematic film "star." Drawing upon the work of a number of different theorists, Gaines posits that the star function comprises "at least three entities: roughly, 'private' person, character role(s), and public image" (33). Allowing for some slight modification necessitated by the documentary genre, each of these entities obtains for the persons presented in *Paris Is Burning*, even though the latter do not function as "stars," strictly speaking.[19] Our sense of the queens as *"private" persons* is achieved through the film's presentation of them, not only in the context of the drag balls but beyond it—at home, on the street, out shopping, and so forth. The "private" status of the figures thus presented to us is, of course, fictive, in that the presentation itself violates the very terms of such privacy, with the result that the "real" persons thus referenced serve only as what Gaines calls an "authenticating presence" for the "star" entity as a whole (33). At the same time, while they do not function as *character roles,* per se, such stylizations as the queens undertake in the drag balls that Livingston showcases do constitute what we might call "performed personae," which become associated with the individuals who present them much as character roles are associated with certain film "stars." Finally, that the queens enjoy *public images* cannot be in doubt, inasmuch as the film itself produces them, either as coextensive with the "performed personae" mentioned above (for those whom the film presents only in the enactment of their stylizations) or as comprising both those personae and the sense of the "private" persons that is (fictively) constituted in the film's "real-life" sequences.

Insofar as they (and the "personal image" that I am suggesting comprises them) partake of the *personal quality* of the individual with whom they are associated, all of the entities identified above as obtaining for the documentary subjects of *Paris Is Burning* constitute objects of torts law privacy and are thereby legally protected against undue appropriation (see Gaines 180). But, of course, Livingston committed no undue appropriation of her subjects' "personal images," since her use of such in her film was authorized by those very subjects' signing of documents that "released" her from liability for such a charge. Consequently, those entities duly became elements in Livingston's own object of intellectual property—namely, the film *Paris Is Burning*—the publicization of which then fully established

Livingston's own creative agency. By this I mean not only that Livingston was officially recognized as having generatively produced the documentary but that that very recognition constituted her substantive intervention in the social-symbolic realm—her effective self-production as (filmmaking) subject. In other words, owing to the specific public character of the mass-media context in which she operates, Livingston achieves precisely what the queens themselves fail to achieve—an agential role in her own subjective constitution: Livingston actively and intentionally produces her film, as a result of whose wide distribution and favorable reception she accedes to the subjective status of filmmaker, with all the social-symbolic significance that implies.

The queens' failure to enact a similar self-constitution must be accounted for in terms of all three of the aspects that they now manifest, as a consequence of their presentation in Livingston's film and their resultant approximation to the star entity as theorized by Gaines. Their signing over to Livingston the right to appropriate their personal images for financial gain effectively exhausted the queens' *actual* private-personal subjectivity since, as we have noted, the minute such subjectivity is presented on film, its "private" status becomes a mere fiction. This fact aside, however, even the putative *"private" persons* presented in *Paris Is Burning* could not manifest such self-constitutive agency as we are trying to identify here. This is because those "private" persons are by definition the persons in which the queens function outside the drag-ball context and thus constitute recognizable entities in the governing discursive social field; in other words, the "private" person corresponds to subjectivity *as such*. As Butler has made clear, the performative quality of this latter actually precludes the subject's exercise of effective agency in its own constitution. Thus, any semblance of the queens' "private" persons that is registered in *Paris Is Burning* and its attendant publicity cannot appear as the effect of their own subjective agency, but only as the product of a discursive process over which they have no control.

The *public images* of the queens that *Paris Is Burning* disseminates certainly partake of their subjective agency, insofar as these images comprise, among other elements, the theatrical stylizations that the queens voluntaristically undertake. Those motivated stylizations do not themselves fully *constitute* the queens' public images, however, since they do not embody the means of effecting their own publicization. Rather, those means consist in the film itself, without which the queens clearly would enjoy no public image at all, in the sense operative here; and the film is produced not by the those whom it presents as its "subjects" but rather through the *filmmaker's* own subjective agency, which thus supersedes that of the queens as a social-symbolic phenomenon.

Thus the only aspect of their personal entities that can be considered an effect of the queens' own subjective agency is the *performed personae* that they produce through their stylizations in the drag-ball context. Precisely because that context—for all its public character—does not enjoy the social-symbolic status that is accorded to the courtroom or the mass-distribution film, however, the activities that take place within it do not constitute substantive interventions in the governing social order. Indeed, for them even to be *visible* in that order, drag-ball stylizations must first be rendered in suitable symbolic terms—a rendering that is effected, in this case, not by the queens themselves but, as I have indicated above, by Livingston, through her film production. The reasons for this are not mysterious but rather are founded in conditions of access to capital that are themselves overdetermined but not unintelligible. As Livingston herself says: "I am educated and I am white, so I have the ability to write those grants and push my little body through whatever door I need to get it through. . . . If [the queens] wanted to make a film about themselves, they would not be able" (Green 11).

What this means, of course, is that, given the conditions they faced, any desire on the queens' part to publicize widely their activities at the drag balls, and thus to achieve socially influential subjective agency, could be addressed only by their renouncing the very possibility of such agency in the first place—specifically, by signing legal "releases" that provided for their becoming the "subjects" of documentary film while simultaneously foreclosing the possibility of their becoming the productive subjects of significant social effects. The only way out of this catch-22, clearly, would be to alter the conditions that dictate it. This would entail nothing other than the queens' amassing sufficient capital to effect *their own* wide publicization of drag-ball practice. The resultant crossing from the localized public of the ballroom to the more extensive one implicated in mass-cultural media would be critical in at least two ways, constituting a decisive juncture in the queens' career as agential social subjects, and conferring on their cultural commentary the "edge" that, in our eagerness to see their practice as subversive, we too easily forget it does not yet possess.

1994

Notes

1. Stewart Klawans, for example, predicts that we will be "impressed" by Livingston's clearly having won the confidence of her subjects, who, because they inhabit "a part of the world that doesn't see many white women, . . . had every reason to mistrust her" (Review of *Paris Is Burning, The Nation* 252.15 [22 April 1991]: 536). This assertion is curious, to say the least, in that it implicitly presumes our identification with Livingston, whose impressiveness must be primarily a function of the degree to which we ourselves would feel alien in the drag-ball setting. More than this, though, Klawans seems to miss a crucial point of the film regarding the significance of white women to ball participants. One of the movie's most startling scenes, after all, features the "petite" Latina/o preoperative transsexual, Venus Xtravaganza, confiding to the camera her desire to be a "spoiled, rich white girl," and thereby indicating that any feelings she has about white women derive not from the fact that she "doesn't see many" of them but rather from her bombardment with countless highly stylized images of them from almost every quarter of the contemporary culture industry.

2. John Howell, "Exits and Entrances: On Voguing," *Artforum* February 1989: 11.

3. Jim Farber, "Clothes Make the Man," *Mother Jones* 16.2 (March/April 1991): 75. The consistency with which reviewers subsume the various categories in which ball contestants compete under the rubric of "voguing" indicates the degree to which they have seized on the activity as synecdochically representative of ball culture. Ironically, in thus rendering generic this one aspect of the balls, these commentators succeed in decontextualizing the stylized dance form in much the same way as did its prime popularizer, Madonna, whom many of them harshly criticize for, as Farber puts it, "poaching" the "subculture" in her song and video "Vogue" (Sire, 1990).

4. Jesse Green, "Paris Has Burned," *New York Times* 18 April 1993: section 9, p. 11.

5. For a useful account of the ongoing problematization and reconfiguration of the public sphere, see Bruce Robbins, "The Public As Phantom," introduction to *The Phantom Public Sphere*, ed. Robbins for the Social Text Collective, Cultural Politics 5 (Minneapolis: University of Minnesota Press, 1993) vii–xxvi.

6. Judith Butler, *Gender Trouble: Feminism and the Subversion of Identity* (New York: Routledge, 1990).

7. Judith Butler, "Critically Queer," *GLQ: A Journal of Lesbian and Gay Studies* 1.1 (1993): 21. A slightly different version of this essay also constitutes chapter 8 of Butler's *Bodies That Matter: On the Discursive Limits of "Sex"* (New York: Routledge, 1993) 223–42.

8. Eve Kosofsky Sedgwick, "Queer Performativity: Henry James's *The Art of the Novel*," *GLQ: A Journal of Lesbian and Gay Studies* 1.1 (1993): 1–16. Sedgwick, too, sounds a warning regarding the misconstrual of Butler's theory, skeptically citing "some of the uses scholars are trying to make of performativity as they think they are understanding it from Judith Butler's and other related recent work" (15).

9. J. L. Austin, *How to Do Things with Words*, the William James Lectures delivered at Harvard University in 1955, ed. J. O. Urmson and Marina Sbisà, 2nd ed. (Cambridge: Harvard University Press, 1975). For their discussions of Austin, see Butler, "Critically Queer" 17–18; and Sedgwick 2–3.

10. Judith Butler, "Gender Is Burning: Questions of Appropriation and Subversion," chapter 4 of *Bodies That Matter*, 131.

11. I am reminded here of the classic children's story in which a young boy's stuffed toy rabbit accedes to the status of the Real within the context of the nursery (analogous to the ball setting in *Paris Is Burning*), by virtue of the child's love for it. When the Rabbit—declared to be germ-infested after the child's bout with scarlet fever—is eventually discarded by the child's nurse and apparently forgotten by the boy himself, the Rabbit's despair is relieved by the appearance of the "nursery magic Fairy" (!), who promises to take him away and "turn [him] into Real." "Wasn't I Real before?" the Rabbit asks. The Fairy replies, "You were Real to the Boy . . . because he loved you. Now you shall be Real to every one." The Fairy's subsequent transformation of the Rabbit into a living animal that everyone will recognize as "Real" corresponds to the social sanctioning of certain "fantasies" such that they become generally recognized as the parameters of normative subjectivity. See Margery Williams, *The Velveteen Rabbit; or, How Toys Become Real* (1922); illus. William Nicholson (New York: Avon, 1975) 38–40.

12. Antony Easthope, *Poetry As Discourse* (London and New York: Methuen, 1983) 44.

13. bell hooks, "Is Paris Burning?" *Black Looks: Race and Representation* (Boston: South End Press, 1992) 150–54. For Butler's commentary, see "Gender Is Burning" 133–36.

14. Vincent Canby, "Aching to Be a Prima Donna, When You're a Man," *New York Times* 13 March 1991: B3.

15. Green's article itself emblematizes the process whereby the official organs of public culture underwrite their own continued hegemony. The piece's headline proclaims that "Paris Has Burned," while the text takes as evidence of drag-ball culture's demise the fact that "the balls, which had moved downtown in their moment of fame, have mostly moved back to Harlem" (11). Purporting merely to register the apparent death of drag-ball culture, by implicitly rendering Harlem as a sort of cultural graveyard in relation to the vitality of downtown Manhattan, the piece crucially participates in setting the terms according to which ball culture is adjudged to be defunct.

16. Samuel D. Warren and Louis D. Brandeis, "The Right to Privacy," *Harvard Law Review* 4.5 (15 December 1890): 205. For a full review of the different legal areas in which privacy is generally recognized, see Vincent J. Samar, *The Right to Privacy: Gays, Lesbians, and the Constitution* (Philadelphia: Temple University Press, 1991), especially chapter 1, "The Objects of Legal Privacy."

17. For an account of the controversy and a defense of Warren and Brandeis, see "The Right to Privacy in Nineteenth Century America," *Harvard Law Review* 94.8 (June 1981): 1892–1910.

18. Jane M. Gaines, *Contested Culture: The Image, the Voice, and the Law* (Chapel Hill: University of North Carolina Press, 1991); see, especially, p. 180.

19. One reason for this is that whatever "public images" they enjoy do not extend beyond the realm represented in and constituted by the film itself.

3 Playing in the Dark

Privacy, Public Sex, and the Erotics of the Cinema Venue

Toilet

Public sex loomed large in the popular consciousness in late 1991, for in July of that year, Paul Reubens—"Pee-wee Herman" of television and movie fame—was arrested at a Sarasota, Florida, adult movie theater for allegedly masturbating in view of several undercover police officers, and the ensuing media coverage was widespread and intensive. Amidst the sensational clamor that characterized this coverage, two things impressed themselves upon me: the fundamental silliness of the charges; and the sense that, despite this, serious questions inhered in the relation the case posited among social regulation, conceptions of public space, and the form and function of the (adult) movie theater. Exactly how these factors combine to constitute the significance of public sex was nonetheless unclear to me up through the resolution of Reubens's case in November 1991, which pretty much ended media discussion of the pertinent issues. My confusion began to abate, however, in the month following that resolution,

Paul Reubens as Pee-wee Herman, in a scene from the children's television show *Pee-wee's Playhouse*. Photo courtesy of Photofest.

when I started seriously to consider just what was at stake in those issues, because I had developed a compelling personal interest in them.

In December of 1991, my lover and I were nearly thrown out of our local Y—the Central Branch of the Greater Boston YMCA—for engaging in public sex, a behavior judged to be in conflict with the mission of the Young Men's Christian Association. No one actually saw any sexual activity take place between us—though, as the following analysis makes clear, the social significance of "public sex" implicates just such a lack of eyewitness observation; rather, the charge seemed to be based on evidence that was not physically visible at all. Having finished our regular swim one weekday midmorning, the two of us—both deeply submerged in a holiday-season funk—stood dressing ourselves at adjacent lockers in the men's locker room. We were alone in the facility—not surprisingly, given the hour—though one or two other members had probably just left the locker room as we were finishing our showers and proceeding to our aisle. While we were dressing, the door at the end of the main aisle, which ran immediately alongside our lockers, burst open and two members of the Y staff strode purposefully into the locker room. They approached our bank of lockers, stopped opposite us (we were nearly dressed now), and stared for a second; we stared back. After a pause of no more than one beat, the more assertive of the pair pointed at us and said to the other, "These two." Then, as he turned and marched quickly back out of the locker room, he ordered us to report to the membership office before we left the building, ignoring Thom's vocal inquiries as to why we should do so.

Our funk now turned to fury—in response as much to the homophobia to which we felt subjected as to the implicit accusation in which it was manifested—we decided between ourselves to ignore the staff member's command, and defied anyone to stop us as we left the area. As it happened, we proceeded unhindered, though it seemed that a number of the staff looked askance at us as we emerged from the locker room. Recognizing the more passive of the two staff members who had approached us stationed behind the service desk, we demanded to know why we had been accosted, and he replied, not at all unsympathetically, that another YMCA member had complained that two men in the locker room had seemed "a little too intimate with each other." "But I saw nothing," he quickly assured us, referring to his earlier inspection of the scene with his more zealous colleague.

At that point our rage left us fairly dumbfounded, but later I became fixated on the fact that the grounds for our detainment consisted solely in the vague description by some anonymous witness of "improper" intimacy between two men, signs of which intimacy—rather than actual physical descriptions of its perpetrators, for apparently the complainant provided none—became the justification for the one staffer's identification of us as the prime suspects; for, while his coworker may have "seen nothing," as he put it, this man certainly saw *something* when he looked at the two of us standing together. The question is, what did he see? Considering this, we realized, too late, what we ought to have said regarding our "intimate" appearance: "*Of course* we seem intimate with each other, we're lovers!" Undoubtedly, though, this information, too, would have been inassimilable to the mission of the YMCA.

Further thought made it plausible to me that what the more aggressive staff member noted when he looked at us was a way of interacting—stemming from the affective and erotic nature of our relationship—that did indeed indicate a much greater degree of intimacy than he was accustomed to seeing between two men, though strictly speaking we were merely getting dressed.[1] Consequently, he interpreted our interaction as the illicit irruption of male-male eroticism into the public space of the YMCA locker room. (I might add, too, that this interpretation probably seemed all the more feasible given the mixed-race nature of our relationship; for a black man and a white man to evidence any degree of intimacy in this culture is for them to verge on the outright admission of their erotic relation.) On the other hand (I wondered to myself) why did it have to be that way? Could it not be that Thom and I were the ones who had suffered the offense? We had, after all, been alone in the room, mutually consenting to whatever apparently improper behavior we were engaged in. Moreover, couldn't the aura of intimacy that apparently implicated us in illicit activity serve, conversely, as a sign of and a boundary around an effectively private realm, ensconced within which we could have legitimately done whatever we wanted with each other—kissed, caressed, had genital sex?[2] And, in that case, did not the appearance of the staff members on the scene actually constitute a violation of our privacy? In other words, and especially considering the range of "private" activities that take place in the locale, what was so necessarily *public* about that locker room after all?

Fortunately for the purpose of this inquiry, I am by no means the first person to address this question or, more generally, to consider how extremely indistinct is the boundary between public and private space. Indeed, when we think about it, so common are the instances through which that indistinctness is made manifest that we need not recur to social-philosophical theory to elucidate it (though I will do that soon enough); rather we can illustrate it by reference to a perfectly mundane occurrence. First, we might note that if the anecdote that I have presented above indicates the degree to which ostensibly *public* places might actually share in attributes of the *private*, so too can spaces that are often experienced as in some sense private be forcefully shown up as effectively public arenas. One thinks, for instance, of one's automobile, secured within which one is likely to feel screened against violation from the outside as one tools down the road, listening to what one wishes on one's stereo, and otherwise in apparent control of one's surroundings—so much so, in fact, that one is not unlikely to take the opportunity, should the need arise, to adjust one's underwear, perhaps, or scratch oneself, or pick one's nose. . . . Until, at least, one arrives at the next stop signal, whereupon one catches sight of one's fellow motorist in the adjacent lane, eyes fixed on one's indiscreet finger as a reminder that one is not alone in one's home—not *really*, in other words, in private. (One thinks, too, in response to this example, of how it is predicated on the idea that one in fact owns a car in the first place, thus indicating the degree to which the enjoyment of *private space*—or even the semblance of it—is, in accordance with the cultural logic of socioeconomic class, a direct function of access to *private property*.)

The example is a simple one—not to say vulgar—but the embarrassment that ensues upon thus being discovered in such an indiscretion suggests the greater danger that can attend the confusion of the public and private realms in its most extreme cases. In order to consider some of those cases—and as a way of approaching the implication of the movie-theater context in the problematic of public space—let us turn to some situations offered by recent films and their peculiar disposition of the issues in question.

Taxi

My point regarding the conventional conception of a car interior as effectively private space is strikingly illustrated in Brian De Palma's 1980 *Dressed to Kill* (Filmways/Samuel A. Arkoff/Cinema 77). The film's enactment of that conception, while somewhat extreme in degree, is nonetheless standard in kind, and in its structure substantially conforms to the scenario I have sketched above. In its initial sequences, *Dressed to Kill* focuses on a middle-aged, apparently upper-middle-class New York woman named Kate Miller (Angie Dickinson), whose intense and disturbing sexual fantasies (one of which we are made privy to in the opening scene) are evidently both cause and effect of the severe sexual frustration that she suffers in her relationship with her husband. After watching Kate discuss this frustration with her psychotherapist, Dr. Robert Elliott (Michael Caine), we cut to a view of her inside an art museum, where she embarks on a rather cat-and-mouse-like flirtation with a man—a stranger—who had been sitting next to her in one of the galleries. Having lost the man amid the labyrinthine museum interior, Kate finally exits the building in exasperation, only to sight him sitting in the back seat of a cab, in front of the museum; as a signal to her he dangles from the window of the cab the glove she had dropped inside the gallery. When she laughingly and apologetically approaches him in the cab, he immediately pulls her into the car, kissing her passionately, and they promptly begin to have sex on the floor of the back seat, ignoring the cabby, as the latter quietly adjusts his rearview mirror in order to get a better perspective on the proceedings.[3]

This subtle act on the part of the driver becomes crucial later on—crucial not to substantive developments in the story but to how we are invited to think about Kate and her tryst, which continues after the taxi drops the pair off at the man's apartment. When Kate finally takes her leave and prepares to exit the building, she is attacked in the elevator by a mysterious figure in a trench coat, sunglasses, and long-haired wig, who stabs her repeatedly and leaves her to die. Later, once her body has been discovered (by a prostitute who becomes embroiled in the case [Nancy Allen]) and the police begin their investigation (under the direction of a Detective Marino [Dennis Franz]), the explicit link is made between Kate's liaison in the taxi and the danger in which she subsequently found herself. Questioning Dr. Elliott about Kate's state of mind on the morning of her murder, Marino suggests that she was suicidal. Elliott responds with a question:

> Do you think she wanted to get killed?
>
> **Marino:** Don't you? Hm? Look, we got some hot-pants broad cruising around for some action. The guy she picked up went down on her in a cab, for chrissake; I got a "blow-by-blow" description from the cabby. After she finishes with him she comes onto some weirdo in the elevator? [His voice rises to suggest not doubt, but rather incredulity at the be-

havior of a woman he has already decided was bent on self-destruction.] Hey, there's all kinds of ways to get killed in this city—*if* you're looking for it.

Elliott: Well. Yes, she did have a problem about her sexual worth. . . .

What particularly strikes me about this exchange is the ease with which sex drive is conflated with death wish—an extremely common popular conception, but no less noteworthy for that, especially given its deployment here as a means by which to render a judgment against the woman who actively seeks sexual pleasure. Let us look closely at how the conversation develops. By way of an affirmative answer (and in direct response) to Elliott's query—"Do you think she wanted to get killed?"—Marino invokes Kate's search for sexual pleasure: "Look, we got some hot-pants broad cruising around for some action." The apparent search for sexual "action" is offered as patent evidence of Kate's "real" mission of self-destruction—as an emphatic "yes" to the question Elliott has posed. In this scenario, the "weirdo" who killed Kate must be some man whom she "came onto" in the elevator, engaging in a solicitation Marino implicitly characterizes as one of "all kinds of ways to get killed in this city." Then, Marino having thus made the direct connection between a woman's search for sexual pleasure and her self-destructive impulses, Elliott closes the circuit, as it were, reanchoring the latter impulses in Kate's sexual distress: "Well. Yes, she did have a problem about her sexual worth."

What I am suggesting is that the danger Kate confronts when she embarks on her rendezvous is actually twofold: first, there is the real physical danger that results in her murder, but which, it must be stressed, is not the consequence of her search for sexual pleasure *itself,* as Marino and Elliott would have it, but of the constraining circumstances under which a woman must conduct such a search in our society; second, there is the danger posed by those who would construe the aforementioned physical risks as the effect not of various social conditions but rather of the woman's psychosexual distress, evidence of which they discern in her very manifestation of sexual desire. In Kate's case, this latter danger takes on a paradoxical aspect, in that it isn't fully expressed until after her death (in the conversation I cite above), and yet it is one of the enabling conditions for the murder itself. I might add, too, that the two dangers' common origin in patriarchically ordered social codes that implicitly prohibit a woman's seeking sexual pleasure is indicated in the fact that not only the interpretation of Kate as psychosexually disturbed but her actual murder, as well, is perpetrated by Dr. Elliott, who is eventually demonstrated to be—in the generally misogynistic terms of the film—the biggest "weirdo" of them all.

What I am most interested to underscore, however, since it most closely bears on my primary concern, is that the full expression of what I cite above as the second danger Kate faces depends on her misapprehension of an effectively public space—the back seat of the taxicab—as a fundamentally private one, and on the way the cabby subsequently corrects that misapprehension when he reports what he saw in his rearview mirror. It is only by means of this evidence that Marino is able to construe Kate as inappropriately sexually adventuresome, and thus to register for the viewing audience the sociosexual ethic that reigns in the world of the film.

Moreover, to reintroduce a consideration I alluded to in my parable about the automobile tour, the cabby's role in that registration underscores the implication of a class politics in Kate's (and her partner's) construal of the cab's rear seat as a private space. That construal obviously must entail effacing the cabby's presence in the car, in much the same way that, for instance, the moneyed aristocrat (or analogously situated personage) effaces the presence of a chauffeur, or

Kate Miller (Angie Dickinson) consults with her psychotherapist, Dr. Robert Elliott (Michael Caine), in a scene from *Dressed to Kill* (dir. Brian De Palma, Filmways/Samuel A. Arkoff/Cinema 77, 1980). Photo courtesy of Photofest.

of the wait staff at table, thus enabling himself to say or do things that would be extremely impolitic were the servant acknowledged to be a conscious human being. In this light, the cabby's character-damning testimony can be read as a sort of revenge for the class-inflected uppitiness that apparently grounded his passengers' disregard, but that the film's gender-political disposition implicitly ascribes specifically to Kate.

However they are eventually played out, then, all of the dangers Kate confronts in *Dressed to Kill* are actually predicated on her failure to negotiate the distinction between public and private spaces, and the tragic consequences of that failure are nothing but the extreme expression of the inherent general risk that characterizes the liminal realm between the two domains. And, of course, that general risk will be expressed in a variety of ways according to (among other factors) a highly gender-political logic. If, for instance, the search for sexual pleasure that entails the confusion of public and private spaces bodes ill for the woman who undertakes it, the same type of search can appear as the very epitome of a man's personal liberation. To locate the risk that I am implying underlies that appearance—without for a minute suggesting that it is identical to that experienced by a woman—let us turn to another early-1980s film in which a taxicab figures prominently, not, this time, as the space in which public and private become confused but as a mode of access to it.

Tearoom

The two venues that I have addressed in the foregoing pages are neatly linked in a 1981 film by German director Frank Ripploh, *Taxi Zum Klo* (Promovision International). "Taxi to the Toilet," as it is usually rendered in English, features as one of its primary settings for action various public men's rooms in Berlin, where the main character (Ripploh, in an eponymous and apparently autobiographical role) regularly participates in anonymous sexual encounters—"tearoom" sex—with a variety of men.[4] Hailed as a landmark (the cover for the videotape of the movie sports a blurb from a *Village Voice* review by Stuart Byron calling it "the first masterpiece about the mainstream of male gay life"), *Taxi* is more noteworthy for its presentation and subject matter (its explicit and unapologetic depiction of gay male sexual activity is unprecedented in commercial film) than it is for its plot, which is actually quite conventional. Schoolteacher Frank (known by his friends as "Peggy") professes, "I radically separate my job from my private life and pleasures," and his principal private pleasure is his extremely active sex life, centered on the sort of anonymous encounters to which I have referred above. He is contentedly pursuing this interest, when, much to his surprise and chagrin, he falls in love with a movie-theater attendant named Bernd (Bernd Broaderup). After a short honeymoon period, the two part angrily when Bernd gets fed up with Frank's continued carousing and sexual exploits, which clash with Bernd's own fantasy of idyllic domesticity. The emotional climax of the film occurs in Frank's classroom after this quarrel, when the students, having been told by Frank that they can do anything they wish this particular day, demolish the room, thus enacting Frank's own catharsis and transformation, which make possible the resolution of the story. Presented in a startlingly abrupt final scene, this resolution is drastically telescoped into a brief printed postscript projected over a freeze-frame close-up of Frank's mirror reflection: "Peggy and Bernd got back together. Peggy lost her job as a teacher and became a filmmaker full-time."

This ending, which is relatively indefinite, nonetheless does suggest some changes in Frank's life—changes that I think are significant for our inquiry here. The key development is Frank's and Bernd's reconciliation, since—regardless of its "alternative" nature in this instance, and despite our ignorance as to the specific arrangements that characterize it—such a domestic partnership is consistently figured in the film as entailing precisely the sort of regulation of sexuality that Frank seeks to repudiate through his tearoom encounters and other liaisons. He insists to Bernd that he won't be bound by "medieval" attitudes about sex, and though at one point he urges Bernd to "join in" his next casual encounter, thus attempting to integrate his relationship and his recreational sexuality, it is clear from other contexts that he generally conceives of the two as fundamentally oppositional. Pondering his relationship with Bernd at one point (we are frequently allowed to "overhear," as it were, his silent ruminations), Frank wonders whether he can be "faithful," while admitting that it would be awful to lose Bernd and that he is "afraid of becoming some old fag who hangs out around urinals." This formulation demonstrates the degree to which Frank conceives of domesticity and sexuality as dichotomous and practically mutually exclusive phenomena. On the one hand, he recognizes in his sexual exploits—his failure to be "faithful"—a grave threat to his domestic situation, that is, the possibility of losing Bernd. On the other hand, however, in admitting his fear of becoming an aged loiterer in the tearooms he implies that his relation with Bernd offers salvation from that dreaded fate, but only because it constitutes a regulatory check against his sexual activity.

Taxi Zum Klo's title sequence presents this dichotomized conception in its most extreme form as Frank, hospitalized with hepatitis (the pre-AIDS-era film presents a veritable festival of sexually transmitted diseases), rises from his sickbed, dons his trousers, and departs from the building in a taxicab, which takes him on a desperate tour of his favorite tearooms in search of sexual adventure. At the same time, however, if in the contrast between the tearoom and the bureaucratized hospital we can discern an apparently fundamental opposition between sexual activity and social regulatory institutions, Bernd's function in the film is to suggest that the one actually implies the other. Indeed, in the scene that immediately precedes Frank's departure from the hospital, Bernd, visiting Frank's room, opines that it is Frank's sexual escapades themselves that have brought about his hospitalization. And the hospital aside, it is precisely through his sexual prowlings that Frank initially meets Bernd himself, who, in his desire for domesticity, represents a restraint on Frank's sexuality. Thus, according to the ethic of *un*restraint that the film espouses through Frank, the primary risk of unbridled sexuality is not that it can result in illness but, paradoxically, that it embodies the potential for its own regulatory check.[5]

And yet, Frank Ripploh's conception of the matter notwithstanding, the gay man's pursuit of sexual pleasure need not be stifled by its incorporation of a regulatory function; on the contrary, the latter can

Bernd (Bernd Broaderup) and Frank/Peggy (Frank Ripploh) survey the crowd in a costume-party scene from *Taxi Zum Klo* (dir. Frank Ripploh, Promovision International, 1981). Photo courtesy of Photofest.

actually constitute the condition that allows sexual activity to flourish in an ostensibly public setting. In order to see how this is so—and to address my initial question about what founds the "public" nature of the settings for nominally public sex—let us turn to the classic study of male-male sexual encounters in public rest rooms: Laud Humphreys's 1970 book *Tearoom Trade.*

Having described the settings and behaviors that characterize tearoom encounters—as well as detailing the macrolevel social conditions to which they respond—Humphreys centers his closing chapter on the question "What's Wrong with Public Sex?" which he addresses by means of an extremely lucid and cogent explication of the problem. First, setting aside the legal codes of the United States as anomalously characterized by stringent antisodomy legislation, he reviews the relatively looser restrictions placed upon homosexual activity in European countries whose laws derive from the Napoleonic code, in order to discover the governing principle that underlies these restrictions. Using the conventional social-scientific terminology, he notes that

> *[t]he majority of western nations . . . provide no legal sanctions against sexually deviant acts as such unless certain attendant conditions are violated: (1) such acts must not take place "in public"; (2) physical force must not be used to obtain consent; (3) parental or other legal force may not be employed; (4) none of the participants may be below what each society considers the "age of consent."*[6]

Then, remarking that "the last three conditions are specifically directed to the question of whether participation is voluntary" (158), Humphreys wonders, "could it be that [the first condition, regarding] the regulation of place[,] speaks also to the safeguarding of consent?" In an attempt to answer this question, Humphreys posits a series of hypotheses centering not on what he calls the "physical visibility" of a given sexual act—the commonsense principle to which I referred in the first section of this essay when I emphasized that my lover and I were alone in the locker room at the moment of our imagined offense—but rather on the concept of "social visibility," which he adapts from Albert Reiss: "First," Humphreys says, by way of providing a definition of social visibility,

> *the settings for sex are socially visible in the degree to which they preclude the initial consent to copresence of those who may be involved as witnesses or participants in the act.*

Second . . . , the more socially visible the circumstances in which any sexual behavior takes place, the stronger the sanctions against violators.

And, in combined form, the more the social setting of a sexual act precludes the initial consent to copresence of those who may be involved as witnesses or participants, the stronger the sanctions against violators. (159)

Finally, then, Humphreys is able to extract a workable definition from these hypotheses: "'Public sex,'" he says, "when perceived as a threat to society, refers to sexual acts so situated as to result in the *involuntary* accessibility of others as sex objects or witnesses" (159). In other words, though Thom and I were alone in the locker room, and therefore could arguably have engaged in any activity we wanted in effective "privacy," the very fact that another person might have walked onto the scene at any moment renders the space "public" according to the criterion of social visibility, and thus legally ineligible as a site for sexual activity.

At least, this is theoretically the case. As Humphreys points out, however, by reference to his actual "field work" in the tearooms, an intruder onto the scene of a typical public encounter between men isn't really confronted with the action itself, since that action is bounded by what Humphreys, following Erving Goffman, calls an "interaction membrane"—a sort of psychic delineation of the social space in which the encounter will occur that is mutually constituted by the participants in that encounter. For their part, those participants have already explicitly—though silently—consented to inclusion in the encounter by making the appropriate signal to any other potential player already occupying the tearoom—specifically, they have exposed their erect penises to one another as a sign of their availability for the game. Humphreys emphasizes that "showing an erection is . . . the one essential and invariable means of indicating a willingness to play. No one will be 'groped' or otherwise involved in the directly sexual play of the tearooms unless he displays this sign" (64). Consequently, whenever a newcomer arrives on the scene of such a public encounter, there is really very little for him to see until he indicates an interest in participating in the action; his very entrance onto the site of the interaction—or, in slightly more regulated settings, notice of his approach by a designated lookout—puts an end to whatever sexual activity might have been occurring. As Humphreys puts it:

> *Intrusion of a new person through the interaction membrane nearly always causes a break in the action. The man entering* must *be legitimized or the game will be disrupted, at least for the duration of his presence. Until the legitimation or departure of the intruder, a sort of panic reaction ensues; play becomes disorganized and the focus of strategies shifts from the payoff [the consummated encounter]—first to self-protection and then to appraisal of the membrane violator. (78–79)*

This is no news to any man—nor, perhaps to any woman either, though I can't speak to that personally—who has ever entered onto the site of a tearoom encounter, with whatever intention as to participating himself. To put it in the now clearly crude terminology of "public" and "private," the nominally "public" sexual encounter is always effectively, though tentatively, a *private* encounter up until the moment that that privacy is broken by a newcomer's entrance onto the scene, at which point, however, the encounter ceases, and the sexual activity that characterizes it is replaced by gestures that, while likely feigned, are nonetheless apparently suitable to the ostensibly "public" nature of the venue. Thus, according to this analysis and in the contexts that I have been addressing, there really is no such thing, practically speaking, as public sex; there is only the deft manipulation—through finely tuned regulatory strategies—of the boundary between public and private such that space is carved out in the former realm wherein activities of the latter nature can take place with relative ease.[7]

Theater

Which brings me, finally, to a consideration of the adult movie theater—site of Paul Reubens's purported crime[8]—as a possible locale wherein "public" sex might be successfully negotiated. Clearly, the adult movie theater is not the tearoom on which Laud Humphreys focused his study, so the question arises as to how applicable to it is his account of the manipulation of social visibility that characterizes the tearoom venue. This question is obliquely addressed in Humphreys's brief consideration of the gay bathhouse versus the tearoom as a setting for sexual encounters. As he points out, "the bath is certainly no less [physically] *visible* than the tearoom; gay bathhouses advertise and sport neon signs, they are presumably open to use by any male, and sexual activity is frequently more obvious there than in any tearoom" (159–60). At the same time, however, Humphreys makes it clear that the bathhouse is less *socially* visible than the tearoom, because, as he puts it,

> *urban baths in America have a sordid reputation. The man who enters knows what he is getting into and part of the entrance fee is surrender of his consent to copresence. There is even a ritual to symbolize this act of will: first, the customer hands over his wallet and watch in return for a locker key and then he is conducted to the locker room, where he must undress under the gaze of others. Thus dispossessed of his identity kit and other defenses, he receives a towel (always too small) and a pair of shower clogs. Of course, he may yet deny his accessibility and refuse to engage in sexual acts, but only by creating a "scene," in which he will be labeled as the offending party. (160)*

The exchange of wallet for locker key in the bathhouse setting is the equivalent of the exposure of one's erect penis in the tearoom in that they both indicate the actor's consent to copresence in the sexual field. The relatively less explicit nature of the signal of consent in the bathhouse is both effect and sign of that locale's relative social invisibility in comparison with the public rest room. It could be argued that the adult movie theater functions analogously to the bathhouse in this respect. Indeed, Humphreys cites "the balconies of downtown movie houses" in general (and we should remember that he conducted his research during the 1960s, when such institutions still existed in major U.S. cities) as locales that require only slightly more explicit consent to copresence in sexual encounters than the baths themselves (162). It would seem that one's very entrance into a theater that screens sexually explicit triple-X features might well be construed as implicit consent to copresence in the sexual encounters that likely take place therein.[9]

In fact, this approximates the argument put forward by Paul Reubens's attorney during a preliminary hearing in Sarasota. In denying Reubens's guilt, Ron Dresnick is cited by the *New York Times* as having maintained that "Florida's indecent exposure law did not apply in pornographic theaters. The statute in question says it is unlawful to expose sexual organs except in a place set aside for that purpose."[10] According to this argument, the degree to which the public recognizes and generally accepts that genital sexual activity occurs in adult movie houses is precisely the degree to which such theaters are sanctioned for the exposure of the sexual organs, regardless of what the statutes might dictate as proper use of the facilities.

The judge presiding in the case, Judy Goldman, rejected this line of reasoning, but as is probably already clear, I don't want to be so hasty. Not that I will necessarily be successful in resuscitating the argument, but I do want us to consider carefully the various conditions that obtain in the porn-theater context before we throw it out entirely. In order to do this, it might be helpful to recall a key element of my experience in the YMCA.

Having summarized and adopted Humphreys's conception of social visibility for use in my consideration here, I would now like to reintroduce *physical* visibility as an analytically useful category. Let us remember that, during my intense ruminations following my YMCA experience, I became fixated on the point that because Thom and I were alone in the locker room, there was no one to see any sexual activity in which we might have been engaged; it was not physically visible. Now, practically speaking, and given that it is only its potential offense to the sensibilities of one who witnesses it that qualifies "public" sex as illicit, it is arguable that, to adapt a Zen koan, if there is no one around to see an act of public sex, it doesn't really occur. That is, as crucial as is the concept of social visibility to the operative definition of public sex, it seems to me that physical visibility—or lack thereof—functions in tandem with it or with other factors to produce what I call, tentatively, the pornographic venue. This venue would be a space that is recognized as a potential site for casual sexual activity that would be suspended at the moment that any of the constituent factors for the venue ceased to obtain.[11] In the YMCA context, such a venue potentially emerges through the coincidence of the "private" nature of the sanctioned activities that take place there—full bodily exposure, elimination, showering—and the low physical visibility that obtains in a relatively empty locker room. In the adult theater context, a pornographic venue issues from the coincidence of the very low degrees of both social and physical visibility that obtain there. The low physical visibility to which I refer consists not merely in the relatively restricted nature of access to the theater but, more precisely, in the relatively isolated condition of each of the patrons occupying the auditorium.

Specifically, both the darkness of the theater and the calculatedly widely-spaced distribution of customers among the available seats combine to minimize the visibility of each patron in the auditorium. These conditions clearly obtain in the mainstream movie theater context as well, though I think that the regulated dispersal of patrons within the auditorium is not so staple a factor in that locale as it is in the adult theater. However this may be, I want to emphasize that it is not the minimal physical visibility alone that produces the pornographic venue in the adult theater context but, rather, this factor in conjunction with the minimal *social* visibility that characterizes the locale, so that within it, individual patrons might engage in sexual activity without the risk of offending other occupants of the space.

Thus, given the relatively socially invisible context of the adult theater, it is the circumstances under which a patron does his looking at the screen—one of which, it must be acknowledged, is precisely the nature of the movie being projected onto that screen—that preclude him from being looked *at* as socially inappropriate and disruptive. It is specifically the peculiar conditions of Paul Reubens's *spectatorship* that would have prevented him from becoming a disruptive *spectacle* in the Sarasota incident, had the police not violated the socially sanctioned invisibility in which his actions took place.[12] If, after all, what is conventionally called "public sex" is actually characterized by its perpetrators' subtle transmutation of an ostensibly public space into a tentatively private domain, Reubens's offense really consists in his failure to effect that transformation; or, to assign responsibility more accurately, that transformation was made impossible by the presence in the "public" theater of undercover agents whose purpose was secretly to penetrate the "interaction membrane" within which any given movie customer might have thought he acted in effective privacy. Seen in this light—and despite his eventual plea of "no contest" to the charge made against him—Reubens's condition at the time of the incident appears as one less of criminality than of haplessness.

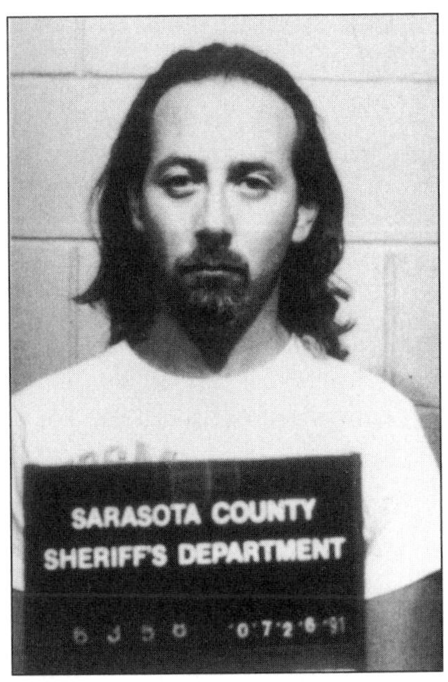

Paul Reubens in the police photograph taken after his July 1991 arrest in Sarasota, Florida. Photo courtesy of Photofest.

However apt my speculations regarding the "pornographic venue" may be in relation to Paul Reubens's specific case—and I, for one, am convinced of their cogency—it is clear to me that the concept requires a great deal of further theorization, and this in at least two different directions. First of all, as my specific consideration of the adult cinema suggests, the continued exploration of the issues I raise here will necessarily engage recent developments, and engender new ones, in film theory regarding the nature and operation of spectatorship in the theater context. Particularly pertinent, I think, is the work of Alexander Kluge on film and the public sphere, especially his comments on "The Concept of the Spectator," in which he addresses the public nature of the film audience. In these ruminations, Kluge emphasizes that "[p]ublic means: access for an indeterminable number of people is guaranteed," and that, should we "try to solve the abstraction of the audience . . . , we would have to pay attention to the fact that the free access for the unexpected, for the late but, nevertheless, arriving extra guest, remains open."[13] Given the always only provisional stability of the viewing audience, in which Kluge identifies its public nature, the theorization of the adult theater as a pornographic venue would have to consider how the individual audience member's effective privacy is to be insured against intrusion by a hostile element—how, in other words, the "interaction membrane" that circumscribes and regulates sexual activity in the tearoom setting might function in the pornographic theater.

Further, however, and more fundamentally, the theorization of the pornographic venue must also entail an in-depth analysis of the regularized manipulation of the public and private realms not just in the locales where "public sex" takes place but in the myriad different contexts of our social life. For, after all, if the mere sight of my lover and me standing together is construed as disruptive in the locker-room context, it might (and often does) appear as no less so in any number of other settings—the street, a restaurant, our own car—whose purportedly public nature subjects us to regulatory sanctions when we are adjudged to violate it. That judgment, and those sanctions, might issue from representatives of state or institutional authority, in which case they will be meted out through legalistic methods; or they might issue from "private" citizens, who as likely as not will express them through brutally violent attack. Either possibility indicates the necessity for us to seize and interpret the meanings of "public" and "private" in a way that enhances, rather than hinders, our free subjectivity. Until that is accomplished, we all remain vulnerable to the two types of penalty that I have sketched above, the difference between which, while deeply significant, is nonetheless only technical.

1992–94

Notes

1. And a good thing, too, since it strikes me as highly likely that my authority to tell this story and offer pertinent analysis in the pages of a serious

scholarly publication derives precisely from my *not* having participated in any illicit behavior in the instance under consideration, which fact goes a fair distance in substantiating one of the implicit points of my argument: the boundaries of privacy are extremely malleable and liable to manipulation by those who enjoy the wherewithal necessary to effect it. In my case, by situating my commentary in relation to a fortuitously apposite and innocuous occurrence—and simultaneously foreclosing consideration of possible other, less "innocent" episodes—I can have recourse to the illustrative details of my "intimate" experience without effectively or uncomfortably breaching my privacy, and thus also (I am hopeful enough to believe) without offending my readers, damaging my professional reputation, or endangering my career.

2. This is one of the points made—as I learned after I hit upon it myself through my rather experiential method—by Richard D. Mohr in his book *Gays/Justice: A Study of Ethics, Society, and Law* (New York: Columbia University Press, 1988). In a section titled "The Inherent Privacy of Sex," Mohr argues that

> *the privacy of sex acts is not only culturally based but also inherent to them. Sex acts are what I shall call "world excluding." Custom and taboo aside, sexual arousal and activity, like the activities of reading a poem or praying alone, are such as to propel away the ordinary world, the everyday workaday world of public places, public function, and public observation. (100)*

While I find it difficult to leave aside cultural "custom" in considering sexual activity (especially when it is compared to what we might argue are the *purely* cultural activities of reading and prayer) and thus to subscribe to the "inherently" private nature of sex, it does seem that, in the cultural contexts into which most of us in the United States are socialized, sexual activity is largely characterized by the "world excluding" quality that Mohr describes. My thanks to David Halperin for alerting me to Mohr's work.

3. For reminding me of this scene in *Dressed to Kill*, I am indebted to Adam Zachary Newton, who tells me that, in his own experience as a cab driver, occurrences such as the one depicted in this film were not at all uncommon.

4. Once again, I must thank Adam Newton for recalling my attention to this film, and for his perspicacity in seeing that my commentary on the nature of public sex would benefit from being situated in relation to both *Taxi Zum Klo* and *Dressed to Kill*.

5. Given this, along with Frank's and Bernd's final reconciliation, it is possible to reconceive the significance of Frank's introductory proclamation—"I radically separate my job from my private life and pleasures." Rather than taking "job" here as a reference to Frank's schoolteaching position, as we must at the beginning of the movie, by the end of the film we can construe it as a reference to his filmmaking career, as distinguished from the "pleasures" of his private life with Bernd. In this case, the new career represents not so much Frank's liberation from the stifling confines of the school setting as the sublimation of his sexual desires—the means by which his errant sexuality can be "expressed" (in the explicit scenes of his cinematic work) and still, as merely an aspect of his "job," be "radically separate" from (and thus unthreatening to) his domestic life.

6. Laud Humphreys, *Tearoom Trade: Impersonal Sex in Public Places* (1970; New York: Aldine, enlarged ed. 1975) 158.

7. This fact has potentially far-reaching implications for our general conception of both public and private "space." As is indicated in the terminology by which we refer to them (and which I myself utilize in this essay), we in effect routinely hypostatize both the public and private realms, conceiving them as discrete arenas the regulation of which thus apparently depends upon the careful policing of their "boundaries." As is indicated in my analysis here, however, those boundaries are essentially fictive, and therefore subject to manipulation the objective of which, when it is undertaken on behalf of institutional interests, is almost uniformly politically suspect. I have indicated in another critical context, for instance, the repressive effect to which the concept of privacy has been deployed in relation to lesbians and gay men, who have frequently sought to use it to their benefit in their fight for legal protection. (See the essay "Private Affairs: Race, Sex, Property, and Persons," printed in this volume.) It seems to me that it is owing to the conventional dissemblance of both the private and public realms' actual nondiscrete nature that beleaguered constituencies often find the concepts effectively marshaled against their best interests.

One instance wherein two such parties have sought to publicize the fictive nature of the public/private distinction—and to negotiate it to their advantage—emerged in Massachusetts in June 1993, when two gay men were charged with "public lewdness" in response to their being observed nude and "intimate" with each other on a privately administered beach north of Boston. In return, the two filed a civil discrimination suit against beach trustees, claiming that a similarly disposed heterosexual couple would not have been arrested but merely ordered out of the area, and that the secluded portion of the beach that they occupied was in effect—and according to existing case law—"private," insofar as it seemed unlikely to be visited by other persons. That various local attorneys have noted the novelty of this argument in such a context indicates the landmark status that would characterize a ruling in favor of the plaintiffs. See Christopher Muther, "2 Men Sue Crane Beach Trustees after Sex Arrest," *Bay Windows* (Boston) 15 July 1993: 3, 10.

8. Specifically, in popular-press terms, Reubens allegedly "exposed himself and masturbated twice during a showing of a heterosexual porno flick" (Elizabeth Sporkin, with Andrew Abrahams and Don Sider, "Pee-wee's Big Disgrace," *People Weekly* 12 August 1991: 67), thus subjecting himself to the official charge of publicly exposing his sexual organ—or perhaps "organs"; the popular media were inconsistent in their framing of the offense.

It is fascinating, by the way, to note the media's obsession—no doubt a response to the slyly gay-inflected sensibility of Reubens's Pee-wee Herman character—with specifying the heterosexually-oriented nature of the films Reubens saw at the theater, as though by doing so they were recuperating as verifiably heterosexual the notoriously sexually ambiguous character of Pee-wee himself. This ambiguity is one of the many issues addressed in the Dossier on *Pee-wee's Playhouse*—Reubens's television show for children—that appears in *Male Trouble*, ed. Constance Penley and Sharon Willis, special issue of *Camera Obscura* 17 (May 1988); the Dossier contains articles by Penley ("The Cabinet of Dr. Pee-wee: Consumerism and Sexual Terror,"

133–53), Ian Balfour ("The Playhouse of the Signifier," 155–67), and Henry Jenkins III ("'Going Bonkers!': Children, Play and Pee-wee," 169–92). See, also, Alexander Doty's response to the Dossier, "The Sissy Boy, the Fat Ladies, and the Dykes: Queerness and/as Gender in Pee-wee's World," *Camera Obscura* 25–26 (January/May 1991): 125–43. For an overview and analysis of Reubens's career as Pee-wee until just before the Sarasota case was settled, see Peter Wilkinson, "Who Killed Pee-wee Herman?" *Rolling Stone* 3 October 1991: 36–42, 140.

9. And here I rush to preempt the objection that this would be the case primarily in gay porn theaters, where the male patrons' implicit acknowledgment of their predilections regarding the gender of their partners mitigates the amount of explicit consent necessary for sexual play to take place. This objection fails to take into account either the extent to which the audience for a given heterosexual feature (which is also bound to be overwhelmingly male) is actually interested in homosexual encounters, or the prevalence in porn theaters generally of sexual activity that, like Paul Reubens's, is essentially solitary.

10. Larry Rohter, "Pee-wee Herman Enters a Plea of No Contest," *New York Times* 8 November 1991: A12.

11. The obvious potential problems with my designation derive from the intense controversy, both among feminists and in the wider arena, regarding the social significance of pornographic material. While this debate interests me deeply—and while many of the same moral, ethical, and political issues that attend the pornography controversy can undoubtedly be raised with respect to public sex—I think that the consumption of pornographic materials and the enactment of public sex have discernibly different significances and therefore need to be conceived and addressed as distinct cultural phenomena. Having said that, I am willing to risk confusion here by deploying the term "pornographic venue" because, in its etymological link to the concept of prostitution, it suggests precisely the sort of nonaffective, nearly utilitarian encounter that I conceive as emblematic of casual public sex.

12. Interestingly, this is the very point made in at least one mass-media consideration of Reubens's case, that by David Denby ("Movies" column, *New York* magazine, 19 August 1991: 50–51). A bemused Denby asks his readers:

> *[H]ow do you "expose" yourself, indecently or otherwise, in a darkened theater? And if you did, and there was enough light to see you, who in the world would be looking? We're talking about a heterosexual porno house, so the other patrons—men, presumably—would be looking at the screen. Answer: No one would be looking; no one except the police. . . . (51)*

Denby then goes on to note that, at his writing, few people had defended Reubens:

> *And why not? He did not solicit a child; he did not solicit anyone. He is accused of abusing only himself. And the location in which he did it, a heterosexual dirty-movie house, is not the same kind of public place as a park or a bus. It is a* private *public place, where men seek solitude. (51)*

Clearly, Denby touches on some of the same issues that I address in this essay, though to slightly different effect. For one thing, while his account recognizes the porn-theater context as a homosocial realm that is a legitimate field for sexual activity, it simultaneously recuperates it as a specifically heterosexually-oriented venue, in contrast to what I have suggested is often actually the case in ostensibly "straight" porn houses (see note 9). Even more interesting, though, are the terms Denby mobilizes in order to effect that recuperation. His references to "a *private* public place" and "men seek(ing) solitude" (which latter condition is achieved, I would argue, by means of the theater's darkness and the peculiarities of audience distribution, which I discuss above) strikingly approximate formulations that one might expect to find in a defense of an exclusive businessmen's club. Consequently, Denby manages to implicate Reubens's transgression (and the transgressive Pee-wee Herman himself) in the consolidation of a highly conventional masculinist social power, an extremely odd—and yet uncannily apt—effect.

13. Alexander Kluge, "Begriff des Zuschauers," *Bestandsaufnahme: Utopie Film: Zwanzig Jahre neuer deutscher Film/Mitte 1983* (Frankfurt am Main:

Zweitausendeins, 1983) 94–95. My thanks to Regina A. Born-Cavanaugh for her translation of this piece.

For more of Kluge's work in this area, see his "On Film and the Public Sphere," trans. Thomas Y. Levin and Miriam B. Hansen, *New German Critique* 24–25 (Fall/Winter 1981–82): 206–20.

For extended considerations of Kluge's work generally, see *New German Critique* 49 (Winter 1990), special issue on Alexander Kluge; and *Alexander Kluge: Theoretical Writings, Stories, and an Interview*, ed. Stuart Liebman, special issue of *October* 46 (Fall 1988).

4 Gay Male Identities, Personal Privacy, and Relations of Public Exchange

Notes on Directions for Queer Critique

The Fetish of Normativity and the "End" of AIDS

For quite a while now, I have strongly suspected that Andrew Sullivan and I inhabit entirely different worlds. For one thing, as the editor of the *New Republic* throughout the first half of this decade, Sullivan seemed comfortably situated within the Washington Beltway, in a realm of national-political discourse and journalistic policy debate for which I feel ill-suited by temperament and unfitted by training. Moreover, the principal testament to his evident ease in that context—his 1995 book, *Virtually Normal: An Argument about Homosexuality*—offered precious little that resonated either with my particular experiences of the homosexual "condition" or with my understanding of its significances in contemporary U.S. culture and society; indeed, I found the general tenor of the volume both problematic and offensive, for reasons that I will elaborate shortly.[1] What solidified my sense of utter difference from Sullivan, however, was an article of his that ran as the cover story in the *New York Times Magazine* on

10 November 1996. Titled "When Plagues End: Notes on the Twilight of an Epidemic," the piece is Sullivan's meditation on what he sees as the substantial advance in the battle against AIDS offered by protease inhibitors, arguably the most significant drug-therapy development since the recognized beginning of the epidemic in 1981.[2] The promise of these relatively new medications, as anyone who follows AIDS-treatment news knows, lies in their evident ability to reduce to undetectable levels the amount of HIV (human immunodeficiency virus) in the bodies of persons infected with the virus, almost universally believed to cause the suppressed immunity that is the signal factor in the development of AIDS.[3] Of course, whether the undetectability of the virus indicates its total absence remains profoundly uncertain at this point, as does the general medical significance of protease inhibitors over the long term. While Sullivan glancingly acknowledges that "there were caveats" to the pronouncements about the drugs' effectiveness that he heard at a summer 1996 meeting of the AIDS Treatment Action Group in Manhattan—affording them roughly a half-dozen sentences in an article that runs to over sixty paragraphs ("WPE" 54)—he is by and large overwhelmingly optimistic about the ultimate effect of the new treatments, hence his proposition regarding the possible "end" of the plague.

Now, notwithstanding my own rather more cautious view of protease inhibitors—attributable largely to my generally pessimistic disposition—it is not Sullivan's relatively hopeful outlook in his article that suggests to me that there is a gulf between us. Rather, it is the fact that he finds it possible to compose the following passage, which I quote from his *New York Times Magazine* essay:

Most official statements about AIDS—the statements by responsible scientists, by advocate organizations, by doctors—do not, of course, concede that this plague is over. And, in one sense, obviously, it is not. Someone today will be infected with H.I.V. The vast majority of H.I.V.-positive people in the world, and a significant minority in America, will not have access to the expensive and effective new drug treatments now available. And many Americans—especially blacks and Latinos—will still die. Nothing I am saying here is meant to deny that fact, or to mitigate its awfulness. But it is also true—and in a way that most people in the middle of this plague privately recognize—that something profound has occurred these last few months. The power of . . . protease inhibitors . . . is such that a diagnosis of H.I.V. infection is not just different in degree today than, say, five years ago. It is different in kind. It no longer signifies death. It merely signifies illness. (54)

We need not consider long to discover this latter proposition belied—and on its own terms. I say "on its own terms" because, while it is arguably true that a diagnosis of HIV infection now signifies illness where it once signified death, it is debatable whether this transformation occurred only with the recent introduction of protease inhibitors onto the clinical stage. Indeed, the status of HIV infection—and even of AIDS itself—as an abiding chronic condition rather than an acute death-dealing malady was emphatically brought to light as long ago as the mid 1980s by the very activists whom Sullivan, in *Virtually Normal*, excoriates for what he sees as their ineffectual "pessimism" (75).[4] On the one hand, of course, that illumination entailed principally a wide-reaching change of consciousness about the meaning of HIV infection, predicated on the very fact to which it also attested—namely that, as Paula Treichler has pointed out, the AIDS crisis comprises as much an epidemic of signification as one of pathogenic transmission.[5] On the other hand, though, inasmuch as that change in consciousness furthered agitation by AIDS activists for stepped-up drug development and clinical trials, it had a clear effect on medical-research proceedings conventionally understood as impervious to cultural critique, and arguably established the conditions for the eventual emergence of protease inhibitors themselves. In short, then, if we are indeed facing the "end" of AIDS, this is due not only to the "discoveries" of medical "science" but also to developments in the discursive field that actually make those discoveries possible.

That Andrew Sullivan is oblivious of the power of discursive formations, however—or, more likely, is unconcerned by it—is suggested by his own syntax in the passage I have cited. In his rush to register the exciting promise of protease inhibitors, Sullivan effectively dismisses any doubt about their ultimate usefulness by positing this doubt as the peculiar disposition of constituencies who are, in his account, emphatically marginal. The terms of that marginality become clear as we trace Sullivan's narrative exposition of the drugs' limitations: having already acknowledged that a generic "someone" "today will be infected with H.I.V.," by the time Sullivan admits that "the vast majority of H.I.V.-positive people in the world . . . will not have access" to protease inhibitors, he has drawn an implicit distinction between these unfortunate folk and those with whom he is really concerned, and he furthers this distinction in his rhetorical aside that "a significant minority in America," too, will be unable to obtain the new drugs. Sullivan's construction here, in indicating the extent to which those denied access to protease inhibitors also populate "America," posits the United States against the rest of the world as the area of primary concern in the fight against AIDS, thereby also rendering those without access to the new drugs—a "majority" of the HIV-infected worldwide—as a functional "minority," whose significance, therefore, must be explicitly asserted, precisely because it is contradicted by the "minority" designation itself. And, in case the full resonances of that designation are not clear, Sullivan registers the vulnerability of U.S. citizens in highly specific terms, noting not only that "many Americans . . . will still die," but that this group comprises "especially blacks and Latinos," the parenthetical cast of the latter phrase indicating grammatically these populations' necessarily marginal status in the narrative Sullivan wants to promulgate.

For what Sullivan wants to say—and wants to say in spite of the sobering truths whose persistence he notes—is made clear in the sentence by which he follows his concessionary acknowledgment: "But it is also true—and in a way that most people in the middle of this plague privately recognize—that something profound has occurred these last few months." The word *but* here clearly signals that what we are witnessing in this article is a very specific process of phantasmic conjuration, which animates Sullivan's entire project. After all, the rhetorical formulation whereby Sullivan first registers the fact of continuing AIDS-related deaths and then announces the end of AIDS in despite of that fact can be rendered schematically as "I know . . . , but . . ."—precisely the formula offered by Kobena Mercer and John Ellis for the disavowal that, as they both point out, founds *fetishism* in Freudian theory.[6] While in Freud's exposition of it as a masculine erotic mode, fetishism has as its fundamental stake the woman's possession of phallic power (so that, as Ellis puts it, the linguistic formula for fetishism is "I know that woman does not have the phallus, nevertheless she does have the phallus in this fetish" [101]), in Sullivan's more specifically *sociocultural* (though not by that token necessarily less erotic) engagement, the stake lies in a rather different direction, as his rhetoric itself makes clear.[7] For if Sullivan can suggest that "most people in the middle of this plague" experience the development of protease inhibitors as a profound occurrence (indeed, even as the "end" of AIDS) while he simultaneously admits that "the vast majority of H.I.V.-positive people in the world"—manifest in the United States principally as blacks and Latinos—will not have access to the new drugs and, indeed, will likely die, what can this mean but that, in Sullivan's conception, "most people in the middle of this plague"

John Dugdale, "Self-Portrait with Black Eye," 1996. Photo courtesy of Wessel+O'Connor Gallery, New York. Reprinted by permission.

are not non-white or non-U.S. residents? Thus, while it may be strictly true that, as Sullivan puts it, his words are not "meant to deny" the fact of continued AIDS-related death, the form that his declaration assumes does constitute a disavowal—not of death per se but of the significance of the deaths of those not included in his notion of racial-national normativity. Those deaths still occur in the scenario that Sullivan sketches in his article, but they are not assimilable to the narrative about "the end of AIDS" that he wants to promulgate,

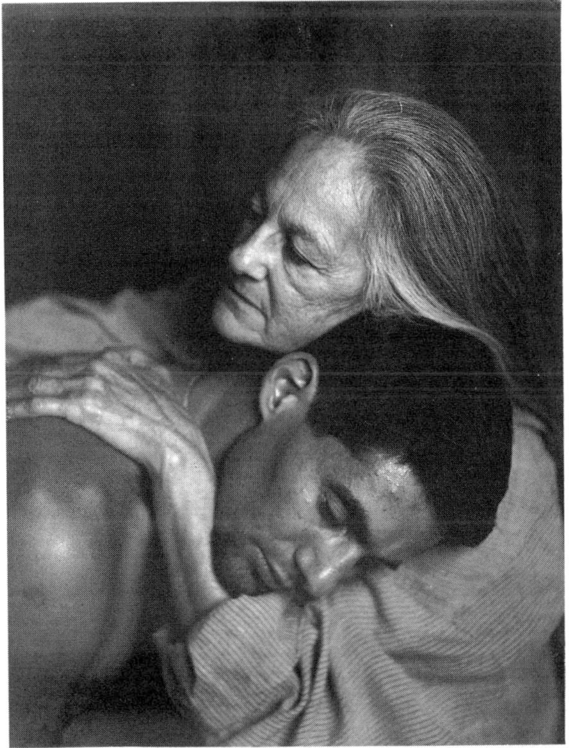

John Dugdale, "The Artist's Mother, Morton Street, NYC," 1994. Photo courtesy of Wessel+O'Connor Gallery, New York. Reprinted by permission.

meaning that, for Sullivan, they effectively do not constitute AIDS-related deaths at all. His disavowal can therefore be rendered thus: "I know that many people who are not white or not U.S. residents will still die, but in my narrative, those people do not really have AIDS"; or, to put it in more recognizable terms: "I know that not all people who have AIDS are U.S. whites, but in my narrative, they are." Casting Sullivan's disavowal in this way allows us to identify as his sociocultural fetish U.S. conceptions of normative *whiteness*, paradoxically figured in his article by a gay male collectivity whose homosexual character, rather than degrading it, actually accords it the purity of apotheosis. (Indeed, this effect is augmented visually by the images that illustrate the article: self-portraits by white gay male photographer John Dugdale, whose striking conventional handsomeness—along with his posing, in one photo, with his mother, who holds him in a tender embrace that signals her all-accepting support—serves to reinscribe the power of normative whiteness even in the face of the debilitating AIDS-related illness that Dugdale suffers.)

Nor is this fetishizing of a masculinized normative whiteness limited to Sullivan's "When Plagues End" article; it also permeates the argument of the book *Virtually Normal,* thus largely founding what I have already indicated is my overwhelming objection to that text and solidifying my sense that, rather than being oblivious of the power of discursive formations, Sullivan is simply untroubled by its conventional deployment. After all, in what is supposed to read as a generous nod to the validity of the Foucauldian theory that Sullivan insists informs recent (and, in his view, misguided) queer activism, Sullivan acknowledges that "it is impossible to read Foucault without being changed forever in one's reading of texts, one's alertness to language, one's sensitivity to subtle forms of control" (*VN* 67). Be that as it may, however, this new "sensitivity" does not necessarily result in one's more careful drafting of linguistic formulations, as is evidenced by Sullivan's own text. In an explanatory preface to his book, Sullivan informs his reader,

I've used the word "homosexual" throughout to mean someone who is constitutively, emotionally and sexually, attracted to the same sex. Although it's somewhat clinical, it's the most neutral term available. I've used the word "gay" to mean someone who self-identifies as homosexual. Both terms are meant to apply to women as well as men. When using the third-person pro-

> *noun, I've reluctantly used "he" throughout. Unfortunately, "he or she," although sprinkled throughout the text, becomes oppressive if used constantly; and the female pronoun, while in many ways admirable, is still jarring to too many people and can distract from the argument. Mixing them up can get even more confusing. So for "he," please read either male or female. (ix)*

Taking this statement at its proffered word (and thereby forgoing a close analysis of what strikes me as its problematical rendering at many points), what are we to make, for instance, of Sullivan's claim, presented a mere twenty pages later, that "much of popular culture, until very recently, was designed to promote views of homosexuals as . . . effeminate" (22), where the received meaning of "effeminate" would seem to belie the putatively generic significance of the term "homosexual"? Or of Sullivan's consideration of the differences between bestiality and "the desire to unite emotionally and sexually with individuals of the same sex; between the desire [*sic*] to copulate with a sheep and with a man" (42), where, depending on who, exactly, desires to "copulate with a man," the impulse does not necessarily imply homosexuality at all? And to extend this interrogation beyond gender-political considerations to racial-political ones, what do we make of Sullivan's claim that "the homosexual person might be seen as a natural foil to the heterosexual norm," just as "redheads offer a startling contrast to the blandness of their peers" (47); or of his proposition that "a social policy which seeks to ban homosexuality has similar paradoxes as a social policy which seeks to banish curly hair" (48), where the imagined color and condition of hair derive their anomalousness in contexts where conventional "white" standards clearly constitute the norm in the first place? The only conclusion that *I* can reach from considering these passages is that, while Sullivan may have been made more "aware" of and "sensitive" to discursive power through his reading of Michel Foucault, he has not thereby become particularly *concerned* about how such power is deployed in the myriad contexts in which it factors, as is evidenced by the discursive testimony to his own fetishizing of identic normativity in the passages cited above. This fetishizing by no means represents the full extent of the problems in *Virtually Normal*, but I focus on it because its manifestation in the book—like its manifestation in the piece on "the end of AIDS"—signals a function for gay male subjectivity that I want to interrogate here. That function is best elucidated through a consideration of the *other* major weakness of *Virtually Normal*, which constitutes an additional peculiarity of both of Sullivan's texts.

Calling Andrew Sullivan

I have already indicated that one of the primary factors in my determination that Andrew Sullivan and I are not generally of like minds is his evident ease in the realm of state-political discourse. It isn't so much the "ease" itself that troubles me, however, as what it signals—to wit, Sullivan's evidently sanguine attitude toward the tenets of classical liberal philosophy. Indeed, the entire project of *Virtually Normal*, as I understand it, is to demonstrate that the homosexual's integration into contemporary Western society—Sullivan's optimal scenario, which itself is telling—can be achieved through the considered application of precisely those conventional liberal-theoretical principles. This strikes me as misguided from the start, but to mount a comprehensive direct opposition to Sullivan on this issue is not my point here. Rather I am interested in the extent to which Sullivan's wholesale subscription to liberal political theory—betraying the bent of his doctoral training in political science—informs the very discursive terms by which he prosecutes even his supposedly properly journalistic undertaking in "When Plagues End." Attending to the dilemma of a longtime AIDS-patient advocate who, he claims, "feels the meaning of his life slipping away" as a result of the impending "end of AIDS" that protease inhibitors signal, Sullivan quotes the man as saying resignedly, "[I]t's a big world and at some point you have to find a way to slip back into it and try and be a happy citizen. What I want is a boyfriend I love, a job that doesn't make me crazy and good friends" ("WPE" 58). Exactly how these latter items constitute "citizenship," happy or otherwise, as the syntax of the quotation suggests they do—and, indeed, why a pleasant existence should be construed specifically in terms of citizenship in the first place—is not at all clear to me. What *is* clear, however—and remains so whatever the accuracy of Sullivan's attribution of this statement to his interviewee—is that the discourse of "citizenship" is precisely the one in which Sullivan himself uniformly engages, particularly when it comes to addressing the sociopolitical significances of homosexuality or experiences associated with it, such as HIV illness. How does Sullivan assert the validity of his argumentation in *Virtually Normal*, after all, but by implicitly contrasting it with the dogma of religious zealotry as an instance of proper civil discourse? Specifically, he avers that "a liberal society . . . engages *citizens* with reasons rather than believers with doctrines" (*VN* 55, my emphasis)—as though the organization of the polity accounted fully for all the possible significances of either social formation or individual activity in any given context. However, that Sullivan does tend to apprehend these latter phenomena exclusively in terms of state-political disposition—and the rhetoric by which he *indicates* that he does—allows us to discern what is really at stake in the fetishization of masculinized normative whiteness that he manifests in the texts examined here.

In considering the putatively natural-law-based antihomosexuality arguments of what he calls the "prohibitionists," Sullivan claims that

*the most humane representatives of this [position] seek to bring people trapped in homosexual behavior back into conformity with what they see as their natural—their true—calling, and re-envelop them in a meaningful and constructive human community. (*VN *21)*

While we must recognize that it is not Sullivan's aim to refute this position on its own terms—indeed, to do so would lead him astray from the line of political-theoretical reasoning that he is concerned to develop—his mode of engaging the prohibitionist stance nevertheless indicates a central organizing principle in his own expositional framework. Granting for the sake of argument the authority vested in "nature" in the prohibitionist view, Sullivan suggests that the invocation of that entity by the apostle Paul, in the condemnation of homosexual activity presented in his epistle to the Romans, implicates not nature as such but the presumedly heterosexual "nature" of individual human beings. Consequently, Sullivan argues, Paul's condemnation could not apply "to people who are by their own nature homosexual" (*VN* 29).[8] This proposition implies that, while he may reject the conclusions of the prohibitionists, Sullivan is willing to accept the principle whereby, as he puts it, homosexuals are to be brought into conformity with their "natural calling." Moreover, inasmuch as he has his sights set on the creation of "a civil culture" grounded at least in part in what "homosexuals and heterosexuals [can] . . . each . . . teach the other" (*VN* 177), Sullivan, too, sees individuals' responses to their "natural calling" as founding their envelopment "in a meaningful and constructive human community." In other words, for Sullivan, answering a "natural calling" to homosexuality is simultaneously to answer an equally exigent "calling" to a productive, properly social function; it is—to put it in rather different political-theoretical terms than the ones Sullivan generally engages—to be *interpellated* as a socially significant subject.

By invoking *interpellation* here, I do not mean to connote the negative sense of constraint that is generally associated with Althusser's originary theorization of the process as an inevitable effect of ideology.[9] After all, the social subjectivities into which individuals are interpellated all entail varying degrees of power and agency, deployable even in spite of their sublimation in an ideologically ordered system. Indeed, my point has to do precisely with the power that Andrew Sullivan is accorded by virtue of his interpellation as a very particular social subjectivity. It is the power to, among other things, rule out of consideration the life experiences of individuals whom he has condemned in their nonnormativity—and, indeed, to undertake such judgment in the first place; and it is granted, I would argue, by his official designation as a properly public homosexual subject.

The "officialness" of Sullivan's position derives not from his being systematically selected as the political "representative" of a given constituency but from his being anointed thus within the realm of serious professional journalism—in the first place by his association with the *New Republic* and the *New York Times*. Indeed, once we recall the status of the press itself as one of what Althusser dubs "the communications ideological state apparatuses" (143), we can see that Sullivan's presentation of a certain mode of white gay male experience as effectively normative is properly an ideological effect, which accounts for both the subtlety and the force by which it is achieved. The specific *principle* operative in its achievement is relatively simple: it is the principle of projection, whereby Sullivan construes his own individual personal experiences as emblematic of the larger social situation on which he has been "called" to comment.

Sullivan's *Times Magazine* article proceeds largely by way of anecdote, entailing primarily his outlining his personal associations with other gay men during the era of AIDS in the urban United States. Indeed, the piece generally grounds the validity of Sullivan's pronouncements on the social significances of the epidemic in his intimate knowledge of one segment of the AIDS-affected population, aggressively presented to us in terms of its potent—if counterintuitive—normativity. Thus we are given a characterization of the photographer John Dugdale as "tall and chiseled, with dark hair and even darker eyes" (58); we are introduced to "Scott, a soldier I had got to know as a 220-pound, 6-foot-3-inch, blue-eyed, blond-haired bundle of energy" (57); and we are shown the restorative potential of protease inhibitors by way of a description of Greg, who has gone from being "skeletal" in his sickness to presenting "round blue eyes almost tiny in his wide, pudgy face, his frame . . . bulky, lumbering, heavy" (60). Identified with these men by mere virtue of his acquaintance with them—which itself already connotes his similarity *to* them—Sullivan emerges through these references as both subject and object of his own representational undertaking, the masculinized white normativity that he projects comprising nothing other than his own subjective status, officialized as "authentic" homosexuality by the journalistic medium through whose public engagement it is widely registered. Nor is this simply a one-directional development, for not only does the journalistic promulgation of Sullivan's experiential subjectivity as somehow normatively authentic enhance Sullivan's own power to construe the significances of various social situations, but his "authenticity" itself provides a cultural *authority* on which the press depends for its continued social legitimacy.

In a sense, then, and without ever having to present a visual image of himself, Andrew Sullivan emerges from his *Times Magazine* engagement as both the effective poster boy for a legitimated gay male experience and as a veritable cover boy for the *Times* itself, which requires his authority as a prop for its own. That each entity, Sullivan and the newspaper, depends on the other for its ability to prosecute an effective public engagement is signaled visually by the cover of the magazine—designed by premier graphic artist Chip Kidd, who, coincidentally, also designed the jacket for *Virtually Normal*, and whose work is discussed elsewhere in the very issue of the *Times Magazine* in which Sullivan's "When Plagues End" article appears. Acknowledging that the design represents an "allegorical vision" of the narrative presented in Sullivan's text (an enlarged, typographically rendered excerpt of which constitutes the whole of the magazine's cover image), Kidd told *Times* interviewer Janet Froelich that he arrived at the idea by asking himself, "What if the type started out sick and then got well?"[10] And, sure enough, the cover presents the Sullivan excerpt in a standard journalistic-press typeface that, at the top of the page, appears muddied and indistinct, but that achieves increasing clarity and resolution as it is deployed down the page through the remainder of the quotation. As easy as it is to comprehend this design as representing a progression from sickness to health, though, it is equally easy to see it as figuring the emergence of a normative, and therefore authoritative, social subjectivity—let's call it "Andrew Sullivan"—

The New York Times Magazine

'A difference between the end of AIDS and the end of many other plagues: for the first time in history, a large proportion of the survivors will not simply be those who escaped infection, or were immune to the virus, but those who contracted the illness, contemplated their own deaths *and still survived.*'

WHEN AIDS ENDS By Andrew Sullivan

Cover of the *New York Times Magazine,* 10 November 1996, designed by Chip Kidd. Copyright © 1996 by The New York Times Co. Reprinted by permission.

from amid the realm of *non*-normativity that homosexual identity is generally considered to imply. Indeed, presented just below the final lines of this "recovered" typeface is the name of Sullivan himself, in a byline for the essay, which the magazine cover assures us will consider what we can expect "When AIDS Ends." Thus while the *Times*, by "calling" out Sullivan as a legitimately representative gay male subject, empowers him to pronounce definitively on a matter whose complexity defies definitive account, Sullivan, by conferring the authenticating seal that his name has thereby become, in return effectively legitimizes the *Times*, and so assists it in that crucial, never-ending endeavor, not of presenting "All the News That's Fit to Print," but of *selling* what it has fitted as news in the commodity that is the paper itself.

Private Subjects, Public Exchange, and the Queerness of Life "In the Open"

Of course, there are other ways of selling newspapers than that undertaken by the *New York Times*, and there are other ways of being hailed as a gay male subject than that experienced by Andrew Sullivan in his journalistic engagement. In the remainder of this essay, I want to consider how certain examples of the former might actually be motivated by certain instances of the latter, which generally promise to be much less benign than the mechanism of Sullivan's particular interpellation.

Take, for instance, the development that occurred in a number of U.S. cities at the turn of this decade, whereby copies of tabloid-style newspapers—issuing from variously-organized editorial and managerial operations and featuring disparate kinds of content—began to be sold at such public venues as street corners and subway stations by a corps of vendors composed primarily of homeless persons. Evidently prefigured by the underground leftist magazine *Street*, which was published in Somerville, Massachusetts, and sporadically sold by homeless vendors in the Boston area from 1986 to 1991, the new breed of publication seems to have been inaugurated with the founding of the New York City paper *Street News*, in 1989.[11] Haunted almost from the beginning by charges of mismanagement on the part of founding editor and director Hutchinson Persons, *Street News* was also distinguished from apparently analogous publications in other cities by its mode of operation, in which Persons—a former rock musician and would-be concert promoter who was not himself homeless—exerted executive supervision over the homeless newspaper vendors, construed as his "employees" within the corporate-structured organization.[12] By contrast, Boston's *Spare Change*—successor to *Street* magazine and published by Boston Jobs with Peace, the same social service organization that published *Street*—was from the beginning edited and managed by the homeless themselves, who were meant thereby to achieve a degree of self-determination within the operation.[13] This difference in the papers' organizational structures is clearly significant, not just because of the differing degrees of agency it implies for homeless persons working with the two publications, but because its raising of the question of agency itself bears on precisely the matter of social-subjective negotiation that I want to interrogate here.

The issue of management structure aside, *Street News* and *Spare Change* actually entered into remarkably similar financial relationships with their homeless vendors. At the time of its founding, beyond an initial supply of ten free copies per vendor, each copy of *Street News* cost sellers 25 cents and sold for 75 cents, with vendors pocketing 45 cents of the difference and the remaining 5 cents going to a housing fund maintained by the paper; by 1995, when its demise seemed imminent, vendors made a 65-cent commission from the $1.00-per-copy price of the tabloid.[14] *Spare Change*, which sold for a dollar from the outset, cost vendors ten cents a copy after the initial free allotment of ten copies per vendor, with the remaining 90 cents being kept by the vendor (Walker; Walters). While the fact that *Spare Change* returned a relatively high percentage of sales income to its vendors may have allowed it to avoid such charges of "paternalism" as that lodged against *Street News* by *Street* magazine copublisher Jonathan Fountain in 1990 (see Jacobs, "Somerville" 26), it is both organizations' engagement in sales operations in the first place that I want to focus on here.

Indeed, it was the distinction between sales—in the form of newspaper vending—and the panhandling by the homeless that it was seen as replacing that received a significant amount of press attention immediately after the founding of *Street News* in 1989. As Sally Jacobs put it in her May 1990 story about the paper, "among some Street News vendors, begging is now disdained and the entrepreneurial spirit is held dear. While no one turns down money from customers in excess of the paper's cost, which they say is frequently offered, they discourage overt begging." And, speaking in the corporate-culture terms that seem to have been encouraged by the management structure at *Street News*, homeless vendor Robert Snowden told the *Wall Street Journal*, "This is my job, and I'm here [selling *Street News* at Manhattan's Penn Station] every day. I'm not asking for something for nothing. The company needs these papers out to the people. And that's what I do."[15] Leaving aside the possibility that the company "needed the papers out to the people" so that it could cover the $52,000-a-year salary then being paid to editor Hutchinson Persons (see Teltsch, "Tabloid"), we should note the emotional resonances of Snowden's proclamations, "this is my job" and "I'm not asking for something for nothing," for it is just such developments in affective disposition—registered here as one vendor's increased personal pride—that both supporters and critics of *Street News* identified as the principal stake in the specific sales project undertaken by the paper's homeless vendors.

Hutchinson Persons himself, displaying an evidently abiding tendency to see the project in terms of vendors' emotional uplift rather than their material benefit, insisted to the *New York Times*, "You can see it in their eyes. Every day they look a little happier. Every day they have a little more self-respect. They are needed, not needy"; in fact, so concerned was Persons with the self-respect of the homeless that he published an editorial in *Street News* in which he suggested that soup kitchens charge 25 cents for every meal they serve, in order to help raise their clients' self-esteem. Needless to say, positions such as this fueled the skepticism about *Street News* that many advocates for the homeless manifested from its inception, with Mary Brosnahan, associate director of New York's Coalition for the Homeless, pointing out that "people don't go to soup kitchens for self-esteem. They go because they are hungry and charging a quarter adds insult to injury."[16]

As I have already suggested, however, critics of the newspaper themselves saw a certain enhanced sense of self as the real stake in the selling of the paper, and this in a way that I think applies as much in the case of the evidently less problematically conceived *Spare Change* as in that of *Street News*. By and large concurring with the judgment of his colleague Mary Brosnahan, Keith Summa, advocacy director for the Coalition for the Homeless, told the *Wall Street Journal*,

> *I think there's something disingenuous about saying that selling papers on the street will help people make the transition from homelessness. I think the only difference between selling these papers and panhandling lies in the way people donating on the street feel.*[17]

In other words, the change in emotional disposition that Hutchinson Persons discerned in the homeless vendors—whereby one could "see in their eyes" an increase in happiness and self-respect—is, for Summa, most significantly registered in those being solicited. Why this should be is actually suggested by the words of one potential buyer of *Street News* who evidently *did not* "feel" any differently about panhandling and peddling, precisely because, in the venue where she encountered them, they apparently took on remarkably similar forms.

While many of the troubles faced by *Street News* seem to have stemmed from questions about the practices of Hutchinson Persons (who eventually left the organization, amid continued controversy about his management),[18] they had their source at least partly in a development that occurred in 1991, when New York's Metropolitan Transit Authority cracked down on all types of solicitation in the city subway system, where the bulk of *Street News* sales had taken place. One commuter who supported that crackdown, Josephine Walker, communicated her exasperation with subway solicitation in a statement quoted by the *New York Times*:

> *I'm sick of it. Every time I get on a train, there's somebody right there in my face holding a cup or trying to force me to buy a copy of* Street News. *After a hard day at work, sometimes all you want is a quiet subway ride home. Is that too much to ask?*[19]

Notably, it is the relational asymmetry implied by Walker's use of the word "force" that, at least in theory, would be obviated in a proper vendor-purchaser exchange, much as that exchange is also meant to obscure the inequity whereby Walker obviously has a home to go to, while the *Street News* vendor does not. Indeed, the reciprocality implied in vendor Robert Snowden's assertion that he isn't "asking for something for nothing"—or in the title of the Boston paper, whereby one receives *Spare Change* in return for spare change—is precisely that which is promised by commodity exchange in capitalist society,

Front page of the premiere issue of *Spare Change* (Boston), 1991. Copyright © 1999, *Spare Change.* Reprinted by permission.

entailing a mutually beneficial encounter between two actors construed as equal because they similarly bear privately held goods substitutable for one another according to the rules of commodity structure. In other words, the equality characterizing the relationship is predicated on a proprietary privacy on which is also founded the very possibility of full social subjectivity within commodity culture. When, for whatever reason, the appearance of such equality fails to obtain—as was clearly the case for Josephine Walker, given her reference to "force" in regard to the vending of *Street News*—the consequent problematization of the relationship manifests experientially as the invasion of one subject's *personal* privacy, as is indicated by Walker's complaint, "every time I get on a train, there's somebody *right there in my face*." This point both suggests what it is that, theoretically, should make one feel differently about being solicited by a vendor than one does about being solicited by a panhandler and, further, leads me back to the consideration of the social functions of gay male subjectivity that I began in my analysis of Andrew Sullivan's professional activity.

After all, if the apparent subjective equality that characterizes proper commodity exchange between private persons precludes such an assault on personal privacy as Josephine Walker suggests she experienced at the hands of aggressive solicitors, then the construal of an interpersonal encounter in terms of commodity exchange evidently implies the increased personal *safety* of the actors involved in the engagement. Homeless advocate Keith Summa suggests that this sense of increased personal safety obtains specifically for the *purchaser* of a newspaper sold by the homeless, and he may well be right, in practical terms, though I am not sure how we can adjudicate this matter in any event. Theoretically, however, it would seem that the homeless newspaper vendor, too, experiences an increase in personal safety, in that the commodity-exchange structure at least renders that person

Vendor selling *Street News* in New York City, during the first year of the paper's publication. Photo by Frank Micelotta for *Time* magazine. Copyright © 1990, Time Inc. Reprinted by permission.

intelligible in a social system that would otherwise not be at all accommodating, and this is no small thing. After all, as we are reminded by the vulnerability suggested in the title of Timothy Donohue's recent account of his own homelessness, to be "in the open" is, by definition, to be at some degree of personal risk.[20]

In a sense, however—and by proposing this I in no way mean to trivialize or obscure the specificity of homelessness—we are all "in the open" whenever we venture out in public space, which is to say that we are vulnerable to various forms of the invasion of privacy that I have indicated is exemplified by Josephine Walker's experience of solicitation on the New York City subway. The variety of these forms derives not just from the range of external factors that might condition any given instance of public encounter but also from the number of ways in which our own personal identities might be perceived by those with whom we come into contact. By way of illustrating this point, let me take my own anecdotal turn, and relate an incident that occurred to me on the 18th of October, 1996. In the early evening on that day—which, to be exact, was a Friday—my boyfriend and I were walking west on W. 3rd Street, in Manhattan's Greenwich Village, on our way to pick up a take-out dinner. As we reached the corner where 3rd Street intersects with 6th Avenue, we were approached by a man who, proverbially enough, asked us, "Can you spare any change, brothers?" to which I replied, "No, sorry"; Thom and I then continued to walk down the street, past and away from our interlocutor. Almost as soon as we had moved beyond the man, with our backs consequently toward him, he hollered out after us, "Why don't you hold his hand if you love him?" whereupon I wrapped my arm around Thom's waist, keeping it there as we turned north on 6th Avenue, and until we reached our destination, two blocks away.

The issue here is not the one that might be presumed from the position of bourgeois guilt—my implication, by my refusal to offer money, in the man's marginalization within the governing social structure. Given the fact of that marginalization—a systemic effect for which an individual's decision whether to offer money or not is wholly inconsequential—the issue lies in how the terms of our interaction were predicated on additional aspects of personal identity that we both discerned at work in the encounter. My responding so emphatically to the man's sarcastic challenge indicates quite clearly, I think, that I took him to be speaking directly to me—logical enough,

I guess, considering that it was I, and not Thom, who had answered his request for money in the first place. At the time, though, I am fully aware, I imagined that the two of us were engaged in an exclusive exchange because both of us, unlike Thom, were black and were visibly identifiable as such. Even when he addressed us in the plural, as "brothers," I considered that I was the one with whom he was really engaged, his term calling me out as a fellow African American even as it conceived both Thom and me as potential donors of cash. In failing to answer to that particular "calling," however, we evidently opened ourselves up for an alternative reading, one that I experienced as working specifically on me, precisely because our shared racial identity implicated the panhandler and me in a tacit dialogue that I understand as always ongoing, no matter what the circumstances. As it happened, our prosecution of that dialogue in this particular instance resulted in no obvious deleterious effects, but it *might* have, precisely because the rules of our engagement were so minimal, if indeed they existed at all. For to be hailed as a gay man, as I felt myself to be in this situation, is by no means a necessarily benign occurrence—as neither is it to be hailed as a homeless panhandler. Which is why, I believe, people go to the trouble to make themselves intelligible in rather different terms—terms that, while not necessarily negating either of these other possible identifications, to some extent sublimate them in useful ways.

What else, after all, did Timothy Donohue effectively do by publishing the diary of his homelessness with the University of Chicago Press? Or, better, what did Lars Eighner do when, in 1993, he published *Travels with Lizbeth,* his critically acclaimed account of his own time spent homeless and on the road during precisely the period when Hutchinson Persons was founding *Street News* in New York City? Eighner himself makes no secret, in his memoir, of his identification as a gay man, acknowledging on the second page that, at the time he became homeless, "I had been writing short stories for the gay men's market for about five years," somewhat euphemistically referencing the pornographic fiction that he had published in such periodicals as *Inches, Stallion,* and *In Touch for Men.*[21] But if that gay identification took a backseat, as it were, to the experience of homelessness that was really Eighner's subject in *Travels with Lizbeth,* both conditions were largely reconfigured at the moment he became a published memoirist, subsumed in his new status as the producer of a narrative whose sale itself constituted his most effective instance of public exchange.

Which is to say that it is not for undertaking a similar project that I fault Andrew Sullivan. After all, who *doesn't* struggle to fit his identity (and I invoke the masculine pronoun advisedly) to the forms that he knows will make it effective, because "safe"? Am I not now writing myself into just such a condition, with the hope of maximizing the agency I enjoy? What I hope *not* to do by thus rendering myself, though, is to write others *out* of the scenario I envision, the possibility of which sacrifice is always implicated in the very power by which I write at all. It is such discursive sacrifice that I have suggested does not preoccupy Andrew Sullivan; indeed, his social status itself would seem to depend on his not giving it a thought. Sullivan's specific example notwithstanding, however, I am convinced that such unconcern is not bliss; further, and also *pace* Andrew Sullivan, I want to conceive of my advocated project of discursive admissiveness in terms of "queer theory," so as to enact a doubly recuperative gesture.

First of all, as I have indicated above, Sullivan himself devotes an entire chapter of *Virtually Normal* to attacking what he construes as "queer revolt" (92)—designated in his volume as the implementation of homosexual "liberationist" politics—seeing it as exemplified in the practice of celebrity "outing" that gained notoriety at the beginning of this decade. Thus Sullivan is able to imagine that, by offering a critique of outing, he is simultaneously exposing the faulty logic of queer activism in general, inasmuch as, in his assessment,

the entire politics of "outing" presupposes a binary state of affairs in which a homosexual is either "in" or "out" of the closet. . . . It is precisely the kind of rigid structure that Foucauldeans [as Sullivan characterizes all "liberationist" or queer activists as being] might perhaps be expected to resist. And far from undermining this structure, "outing" actually perpetuates it. It depends upon the kind of discourse in which something hidden is revealed, something shameful exposed, something secret stigmatized. In order for the punishment to work, in order for the act of outing to have its shock effect, it has to buy into the feelings of horror and guilt that it wishes to resist. It has to make the outed person feel terrified and ashamed. . . . (78–79)

To some degree—and from a certain perspective—this characterization of outing is accurate; but to the degree that it *is* accurate, we might say that it is not a critique of *queer* practice at all, since the extent to which outing implicates a queer impulse is contingent and variable, as Douglas Crimp has cogently suggested. Attending to the specific contexts within which the first instances of outing were perpetrated (by Michelangelo Signorile, then features editor at the now defunct weekly *Outweek*), Crimp points out that

Signorile appeared initially to want to say something about the privileged position of gossip in our culture's management of the *open secret. Outing is not (at least not at first) the revelation of that secret, but the revelation that the secret was no secret at all. That was the scandal of* Outweek's *Malcolm Forbes cover story, for which* Time *and* Newsweek*—not* Outweek*—invented the term "outing." The dominant media heaped fear and loathing upon Signorile,* Outweek, *and queers generally, not because Forbes's homosexuality had been revealed, but because their own complicity in concealing it had been revealed. Forbes was not "outed," the media's homophobia was.*[22]

In this instance, then, the binary logic according to which one is either "in" or "out" of the closet is deployed *against* itself, by way of exposing a primary factor in its hegemony—the "mainstream" media that, as Crimp points out, largely set the terms for the popular understanding of sexual politics in the first place. It is this critical assault on those terms (of which binaristic categorizations themselves are key instances) that should be seen as constituting a queer intervention, one not necessarily comprised in outing per se. Indeed, as Crimp makes clear, outing lost its analytical leverage the minute it forsook this project of queer critique and resorted to the binaristically ordered logic of personal "exposure" by which the major media made sense of the tactic (307).[23] Inasmuch as queer practice entails a challenge rather than a capitulation to operative categories of social-subjective discipline, its objective is not, as Sullivan suggests, "the redefinition of what is normal" (*VN* 91) but the deconstructive interrogation of the concept itself. In order to achieve this, queer analysis must allow for all the disparate factors comprised in the registration of various social identities and in their adjudication against the standard of social normativity—an openness that I would argue *defines* queer engagement in the first place.

Lauren Berlant and Michael Warner have conceptualized this openness by proposing that "queer commentary . . . aspires to create publics . . . that . . . make available different understandings of membership at different times" and, accordingly, "has refused to draw boundaries around its constituency"—a theorization that I find useful precisely because it posits the public not in terms of the all-inclusiveness and, hence, implicit closure suggested by the Habermasian model but in terms of the contingency evoked in the work of Oskar Negt and Alexander Kluge;[24] indeed, Berlant and Warner fairly echo Kluge's assessment of the public character of the cinema audience as entailing continued "free access for the unexpected, for the late but, nevertheless, arriving extra guest" in their suggestion that queer commentary "keep[s] the door ajar" to admit for the ongoing reconfiguration of an academic public (348).[25] This conception accommodates both the unpredictability that I have suggested characterizes public space and the discursive admissiveness that I am insisting must characterize queer critical practice, which would also recognize the implication within itself of public-spatial problematics.

The great promise of queerness, after all, lies in its potential to conceive and mobilize modes of social subjectivity not accounted for in advance by the structures entailed in ideological narratives—that is, to render effectively negotiable the "open" of the public arena, not by simply conceiving the latter as a site for the free play of multiplicitous subjectivities but by consciously deploying it as a constitutive element within subjective identification itself. This is exactly the project that Berlant and Elizabeth Freeman have suggested was exemplified in, for instance, "Queer Nights Out"—collective actions carried out under the aegis of Queer Nation in the early 1990s, wherein participants appropriated to their own queer-inflected uses public spaces and social rituals generally considered the rightful province of heteronormative constituencies.[26] At the same time, though, Berlant and Freeman note about those early interventions what seems still to be all too true about queer critical practice, even today—that is, "the masculine a priori that dominates" queer action, and "the relative weakness with which economic, racial, ethnic, and non-American cultures have been enfolded into queer counterpublicity" (215). I cite these observations not only for the obvious reason that they *are*, unfortunately, still apt today but also because they succinctly present the terms of social differentiation in whose name, too, I want to recuperate the project of "queer theory," by suggesting that such work is "queer" only to the extent that it takes into account this whole constellation of factors—in addition to and in their

imbrication with sexual object-choice—as it interrogates the function of subjective identification in the socially constitutive activity of public exchange.

This is not at all to suggest that every individual example of queer commentary must achieve some ideal full engagement with the myriad factors that make up any instance of subjective registration—or, indeed, that such achievement is even possible; what Berlant and Warner rightly call queer theory's "radically anticipatory" character means that its reach will necessarily always exceed its grasp, which is exactly why membership in a critical queer public is, as Berlant and Warner put it, "a matter of aspiration" rather than "the expression of an identity" (344). On the other hand, though, some aspirations are more valid and realistic than others, and a critical enterprise whose animating concerns imply a necessary challenge to identic fixity cannot be considered in any way cogent so long as it conceives "sexual orientation" as a primary identificatory principle, uninflected by the pressures of other subjectivizing factors.[27] These factors themselves, in other words, must be conceived as aspects of queerness, as Eve Kosofsky Sedgwick has suggested in her assertion that "a lot of the most exciting recent work around 'queer' spins the term outward along dimensions that can't be subsumed under gender and sexuality at all," including "race, ethnicity, [and] postcolonial nationality" (8–9).

Sedgwick's implicit reference to a critical mass of "recent work" in this mode would seem to belie my claim that contemporary queer practice takes insufficient account of the factors she enumerates, except that the intellectuals whose work she cites by way of example—Isaac Julien, Gloria Anzaldúa, Richard Fung—have made their principal interventions via a mode of creative production whose receivedly "artistic" character renders problematic its status within the academic milieu where queer theory currently enjoys its maximum effect. (Indeed, this situation seems to obtain disproportionately for intellectuals of color in the North American context, which raises a whole set of questions that it is not possible to address adequately here.) This is why, in repeating Sedgwick's citation of exemplary queer analysis now, I would point to work that has appeared since her remarks were published, such as Darieck Scott's critique of the deployment of identity politics in the construction of black gay male sexual life, José Esteban Muñoz's theorizing of *disidentification* as a critical strategy in the work of Jean-Michel Basquiat and Vaginal Creme Davis, and Robert Reid-Pharr's consideration of the significance of racial difference in sexual encounters between black and white men.[28] But while this work *does* seem to me exemplary, it is by no means enough; rather, it indicates a direction that needs to be pursued by queer commentary in every instance, if we are to achieve a maximally useful understanding of how subjective identification functions in process, without which queer theory's challenge to identic fixity cannot be effectively realized.[29]

What I am demanding, then, is for those who would aspire to engage in queer commentary to discern the object of their aspiration in such work as is exemplified by the instances cited above, which effectively queer sexual orientation itself by demonstrating how other factors—particularly race—problematize its claim to order subjective identity.  The work I have referenced, in other words, makes the same appeal to the would-be queer commentator that Berlant and Freeman suggest is made by queer counterpublicity to the heteronormative subject, summed up for them in the title of Deee-Lite's 1990 song, "Try Me On . . . I'm Very You" (208).[30] The shift in subjective identification that would be entailed in answering this appeal indicates exactly why, as I note above, unconcern with the deployment of discursive power is not bliss, since it implies a key lesson of queer theory itself—that what is Other to us today, we may well *be* tomorrow, by virtue of an adjustment in conceptual orientation that makes Otherness as we know it unintelligible and, hence, obsolete. Given this, conscious and responsible discursive engagement is an act not of charity or altruistic beneficence but of reflexive interest in a personal self whose limits are conceived as uncertain, at the least. The difference between these two varieties of engagement is precisely the difference between the undignified practice of speaking for others and a much more unsettling—but more exigent—undertaking: my considering Andrew Sullivan, swallowing my contempt, and concluding, There, but for the current discursive hegemony, am I. Queer indeed, and more than a little disturbing; but no one ever said social change would be pleasant, only that the alternative is not one at all.

1997

Notes

1. Andrew Sullivan, *Virtually Normal: An Argument about Homosexuality* (1995; New York: Vintage, 1996). Hereafter cited in the text as *VN*.

2. Andrew Sullivan, "When Plagues End: Notes on the Twilight of an Epidemic," *New York Times Magazine* 10 November 1996: 52–62+. Hereafter cited in the text as "WPE."

3. The most prominent dissenter regarding the proposed role of HIV in the etiology of AIDS is University of California-Berkeley biologist Peter Duesberg, who has generated an enormous amount of published material in his fight against received opinion on the matter. See the collection of Duesberg's scientific-journal articles, *Infectious AIDS: Have We Been Misled?* (Berkeley, Calif.: North Atlantic Books, 1995); the volume of variously-authored essays that he edited, *AIDS: Virus- or Drug Induced?* (Dordrecht; Boston: Kluwer Academic Publishers, 1996); and his magnum opus, *Inventing the AIDS Virus* (Washington, D.C.: Regnery, 1996).

4. See, in general, chapter 2 of *Virtually Normal*. For examples of these activists' work, see Max Navarre, "Fighting the Victim Label," and the "PWA

Coalition Portfolio," in *AIDS: Cultural Analysis/Cultural Activism*, ed. Douglas Crimp, special issue of *October* 43 (Winter 1987): 143–46 and 147–68.

5. See Paula A. Treichler, "AIDS, Homophobia, and Biomedical Discourse: An Epidemic of Signification," in Crimp, *AIDS: Cultural Analysis/Cultural Activism*, 31–70.

6. Kobena Mercer, "Imaging the Black Man's Sex" (1986), in "Reading Racial Fetishism," chapter 6 of *Welcome to the Jungle: New Positions in Black Cultural Studies* (New York: Routledge, 1994) 184. For John Ellis's original formulation, see his article "Photography/Pornography/Art/Pornography," *Screen* 21.1 (Spring 1980): 100.

7. Freud fully theorizes fetishism in "Fetishism" (1927), *The Standard Edition of the Complete Psychological Works of Sigmund Freud*, trans. James Strachey, vol. 21 (London: Hogarth, 1961) 147–57. He also addresses the phenomenon in his discussion of the "splitting of the ego" as characteristic of the neuroses, which appears in *An Outline of Psycho-Analysis* (1940 [1938]), *Standard Edition*, vol. 23 (1964) 202–4.

8. The New Testament passage in question is Romans 1.18–32.

9. Louis Althusser, "Ideology and Ideological State Apparatuses (Notes towards an Investigation)," in *Lenin and Philosophy and Other Essays*, trans. Ben Brewster (New York: Monthly Review Press, 1971); see especially 171–83.

10. Janet Froelich, "Cover Boy," *New York Times Magazine* 10 November 1996: 51.

11. Sam Roberts, "Their Own Paper Gives Homeless Money and More," *New York Times* 8 January 1990: B1. On *Street* magazine, see Sally Jacobs, "Somerville Paper Touts a Prior Claim to Street Beat," *Boston Globe* 2 July 1990: 15, 26. In addition to *Street News* and Boston's *Spare Change*, discussed below, similar papers in other U.S. cities include Chicago's *StreetWise* and San Francisco's *Street Sheet*.

12. Kathleen Teltsch, "Tabloid Sold by the Homeless Is in Trouble," *New York Times* 24 May 1990: B1.

13. See Adrian Walker, "Boston Diary: Spare Change for Sale," *Boston Globe* 6 April 1992: 21–22; and Laurel Shaper Walters, "'Spare Change' Helps Homeless," *Christian Science Monitor* 4 June 1992: 12.

14. On *Street News*'s original price structure, see Sally Jacobs, "News Is Uplifting for Homeless in N.Y.," *Boston Globe* 7 May 1990: 1, 7. On later pricing arrangements and for commentary on the uncertainty the paper faced by 1995 (an uncertainty that was evidently eventually resolved, for the publication is still available in New York City as of this writing, in April 1997), see *Street News* Fall 1995; James Barron, "Street News, Sold by Poor, Falls on Hard Times Itself," *New York Times* 21 December 1994: B3; Shawn McAllister, "Street News May Fold," *Editor and Publisher* 25 February 1995: 16–17; and Matthew Leone, "Bye Bye *Street News*?" *Columbia Journalism Review* May/June 1995: 22.

15. Jacobs, "News Is Uplifting" 7; Christine McAuley, "Liza Minelli Sells Well, Particularly in Subway Trains," *Wall Street Journal* 27 February 1990: A1.

16. Teltsch, "Tabloid Sold by the Homeless" B1.

17. McAuley, "Liza Minelli Sells Well" A12.

18. Kathleen Teltsch, "Editor of Street News Steps Down," *New York Times* 10 June 1990: section 1, p. 36.

19. Calvin Sims, "Subway Peddler Ouster Cheered and Jeered," *New York Times* 18 April 1991: B1.

20. Timothy E. Donohue, *In the Open: Diary of a Homeless Alcoholic* (Chicago: University of Chicago Press, 1996).

This is not to suggest that the vendor-purchaser relationship is never characterized by the real vulnerability of the vendor, the purchaser, or both, but that, according to the tenets of commodity capitalism, that vulnerability is not a *systemic* effect.

21. Lars Eighner, *Travels with Lizbeth: Three Years on the Road and on the Streets* (New York: St. Martin's, 1993). A good deal of Eighner's erotic fiction has been published in volume form under the Badboy imprint of Masquerade Books, New York. See, for instance, *B.M.O.C.* (1993), *Bayou Boy* (1993), *American Prelude* (1994), and *Whispered in the Dark and Other Stories* (1995).

22. Douglas Crimp, "Right On, Girlfriend!" in *Fear of a Queer Planet: Queer Politics and Social Theory*, ed. Michael Warner for the Social Text Collective, Cultural Politics 6 (Minneapolis: University of Minnesota Press, 1993) 307.

23. For a full account and analysis of outing, see Larry Gross, *Contested Closets: The Politics and Ethics of Outing* (Minneapolis: University of Minnesota Press, 1993).

24. Lauren Berlant and Michael Warner, "Guest Column: What Does Queer Theory Teach Us about *X?*" *PMLA* 110.3 (May 1995): 344, 345.

On the public sphere, see Jürgen Habermas, *The Structural Transformation of the Public Sphere: An Inquiry into a Category of Bourgeois Society*, trans. Thomas Burger, with Frederick Lawrence, Studies in Contemporary German Social Thought (Cambridge: MIT Press, 1989); and Oskar Negt and Alexander Kluge, *Public Sphere and Experience: Toward an Analysis of the Bourgeois and Proletarian Public Sphere*, trans. Peter Labanyi, Jamie Owen Daniel, and Assenka Oksiloff, Theory and History of Literature 85 (Minneapolis: University of Minnesota Press, 1993).

25. Alexander Kluge, "Begriff des Zuschauers," *Bestandsaufnahme: Utopie Film: Zwanzig Jahre neuer deutscher Film/Mitte 1983* (Frankfurt am Main: Zweitausendeins, 1983) 95. Translated for citation by Regina A. Born-Cavanaugh.

26. Lauren Berlant and Elizabeth Freeman, "Queer Nationality," in Warner, *Fear of a Queer Planet*, 207–8.

27. Eve Kosofsky Sedgwick offers a useful characterization of queerness in terms of what I conceive as identic "non-fixity" in "Queer and Now," *Tendencies*, Series Q (Durham, N.C.: Duke University Press, 1993); see especially 5–9.

28. Darieck Scott, "Jungle Fever? Black Gay Identity Politics, White Dick, and the Utopian Bedroom," *GLQ: A Journal of Lesbian and Gay Studies* 1.3 (1994): 299–321; José Esteban Muñoz, "Famous and Dandy Like B. 'n' Andy: Race, Pop, and Basquiat," in *Pop Out: Queer Warhol*, ed. Jennifer Doyle, Jonathan Flatley, and Muñoz, Series Q (Durham, N.C.: Duke University Press, 1996) 144–79; and "'The White to Be Angry': Vaginal Davis's Terrorist Drag," in *Queer Transexions of Race, Nation, and Gender*, ed. Phillip Brian Harper, Anne McClintock, José Esteban Muñoz, and Trish Rosen, special double issue of *Social Text* 52/53 (15.3–4; Fall/Winter 1997): 80–103; Robert F. Reid-Pharr, "Dinge," in *Queer Acts*, ed. José Esteban

Muñoz and Amanda Barrett, special issue of *Women and Performance* 16 (8.2; 1996): 75–85.

29. For the fullest recent elaboration of the processual character of subjective identification, and of its modes and significances, see Diana Fuss, *Identification Papers* (New York: Routledge, 1995).

30. Deee-Lite, "Try Me On . . . I'm Very You," *World Clique*, (Elektra, 1990).

5 "Take Me Home"

Location, Identity, Transnational Exchange

—for Jonathan

Entrée

A funny thing happened across from Byzantium, the moderately upscale, vaguely nouvelle cuisinerie located on Toronto's Church Street corridor, at which I enjoyed a leisurely dinner with my friend and colleague Ricardo Ortíz, during the Modern Language Association convention in December 1997. Earlier that same day I had delivered a paper in which I pondered the sociocultural significances of my exchange with a panhandler on a Manhattan sidewalk in the fall of 1996, shoehorning the presentation amid a welter of interviews with candidates for a faculty position in my home department.[1] Thus finished with the stereotypically hectic official portion of my MLA experience, I was ready and eager for the debauch of sophistication that the "Byzantium" rubric would lead one to expect. Having exited the establishment at about 11:00 with my desires in this vein reasonably well satisfied (the food was delicious though the service was poor, the drinks rather meager but the company divine), I left my dinner partner at the nearest street corner and traversed the road to use the ATM in the bank opposite the restaurant—situated squarely "in the gay section" of town, as Ricardo had so helpfully informed our cab driver when asked to provide directions to the place.

Immediately after stepping onto the curb, I was peremptorily beckoned by a man standing just before the entrance to the bank, whose cash machine, I could see from the sign in its window, did not accept the card I was carrying. Evidently in his mid-to-late thirties and thus similar to me in age, the man appeared simultaneously unlike me in a number of key respects—white and pale-skinned with a reddish-brown beard, hair hanging straight to just above his shoulders. With his lean, average-sized frame draped in a somewhat worn overcoat, he presented overall a vaguely rough aspect to which I responded with intense ambivalence, powerfully attracted to the masculinity it figured while wary of the desperateness I feared it might signal. Momentarily stymied in negotiating this quandary, I finally motioned for *him* to come over to *me*, on the logic that the open expanse of the sidewalk was safer than the more obscure territory next to the building.

Taking me up on this suggestion, the man walked briskly toward me, his hands uplifted in a palms-outward gesture of benignity as though to validate the announcement he made: "I am not a panhandler," he proclaimed. "People always think I'm a panhandler, but I'm not. Can I just tell you my story?" Having gotten my assent to this request, he proceeded to explain that he did not live in Toronto but was here visiting a man whom he had met several weeks before, in his own hometown. Shortly after he arrived at the man's home, however, the two of them had a fight and he, my interlocutor, had been kicked out of the house. Now without either his money or his clothes, he was simply trying to raise enough cash to buy a drink at the bar a few doors down the block; did I have any money that I could spare?

I explained to him that I, too, was from out of town, and in fact had just over enough Canadian money to pay for the cab ride back to my hotel. "Where are you from?" he asked. "New York," I told him. "And who are you here with?" I paused for a moment, not entirely understanding the question, and finally said, "I'm here for a convention." "No," he said. "I mean, are you here with your boyfriend or lover?" "No," I answered, "my boyfriend is back in New York." "Oh," he said, without missing a beat, "then why don't you take me home with you?"

My immediate thought, as I later told not only Ricardo but anyone who would listen, was, "I see. You're *not* a panhandler; you're a hustler!" I didn't say this, however. Rather, having become quite a bit more nervous after concluding that he *was* in fact a hustler, I told him that I didn't think that would be a good idea, but that I had two dollars in coin that I could give him, whereupon I handed over the money and promptly hailed a taxi, in which I tried to regroup as I headed back to my hotel.

Even as I attempted simultaneously to gather my wits and gauge the cost of the ride, I was aware that my adrenaline rush issued from factors more complex than usual. Deriving not merely from the simple mix of arousal and uncertainty that I normally experience during spontaneous flirtations, my apprehension went far beyond the question of whether the other man really reciprocates my interest, which regularly addles my senses in such instances. This time, because the man seemed to imply that he was willing to have sex with me specifically as a means of obtaining money—which registered definitively as his primary objective—I worried about *what else* he might be willing to do, the resultant panic impelling me headlong toward my lodging . . . or so I told myself for many months afterward.

Eventually, however, while granting the fear that the peculiar circumstances had undeniably engendered, I was forced to admit that the situation was even more complicated than I had allowed. Indeed, not only had my wonted anxiety regarding my acquaintance's attraction to me clearly figured in my reactions in the encounter, it had actually been intensified by the man's manifestation of his financial interest, and thus crucially contributed to my abrupt departure from the scene. Exactly how this is so strikes me as having import far beyond the petty realm of my own personal experience, which is why I give it extended consideration in the analysis that follows. First, however, I want to indicate one additional factor in the confusion I suffered during my interview on the street, since it conjoins with what I have already detailed to produce effects of more than local interest.

In her landmark 1973 narrative poem, "A Woman Is Talking to Death," Judy Grahn registers the crisis of civil subjectivity experienced by her first-person protagonist when she is asked to bear witness for a black male motorist wrongfully accused of murder after accidentally colliding with a reckless white motorcyclist:

> *that same week I looked into the mirror*
> *and nobody was there to testify;*
> *how clear, an unemployed queer woman*
> *makes no witness at all,*
> *nobody at all was there for*
> *those two questions: what does*
> *she do, and who is she married to?*[2]

While my own situation was obviously much less dire than the one Grahn addresses, and did not at all entail the profound sense of nonentity that is indicated in her poem—partly because I was not being called to account in the context of official state proceedings—these lines were nevertheless brought to my mind by the uncertainty I felt in response to two questions that had been posed to me: (A) Who are you here with? and (B) Why don't you take me home with you? From one perspective, of course, that uncertainty is completely unintelligible, since I did in fact know the answers to these queries: (A) Nobody, and (B) Because I'm afraid to. And yet, my not offering the man this latter explanation was not the result merely of my being loath to manifest my fear, though this factor did indeed influence my course; rather, I was for a moment genuinely confounded by his reference specifically to my "home."

After all, to put it simplistically, I had just made it clear that I wasn't actually *at* home, but as much a stranger in town as he was, though evidently with a less tenuous hold on the rudiments of domesticity to which one generally turns for comfort when one travels. Yet, I probably would have been less likely to forget my advantage in this regard—and thus more apt to recognize immediately what on some level I knew all along: that he had invoked "home" in a figurative manner, to refer to that place where I expected next to bed down—had my sense of locational propriety not already been disturbed by an experience I had undergone the preceding day.

Having presented myself at the airport customs desk after my flight from New York City landed in Toronto, I had stupidly tried to verify my U.S. citizenship by offering for inspection my New York State driver's license. "This," the understandably weary-seeming official informed me, "doesn't prove anything except that you are authorized to operate a motor vehicle." "But it's all I have on me," I protested weakly. To which she replied, "Well, you're going to need more than that to get back into the U.S. Are you traveling to Canada for business or pleasure?" "I'm here to attend a convention," I said. "What is the name of the convention?" she asked, her query immediately registering as a trick question, since suspended from the ceiling just above her head was an enormous electric zipper sign that ran the length of the customs counter, proclaiming in emphatically crimson lights, "WELCOME, MODERN LANGUAGE ASSOCIATION OF AMERICA." "The

Modern Language Association," I said, worried now that I must appear completely illegitimate. "Are you making a presentation at this convention?" "Yes." Assured that my stay would be a short one, she ushered me through the gate, reminding me that I had better be able to produce a passport or birth certificate when I tried to return home two days later.

This problem was never far from my consciousness throughout most of my sojourn in Toronto, and it was brought abruptly to the fore by the inquiries of my new acquaintance as to the whereabouts of both my domicile and my boyfriend, since even as we spoke my birth certificate was supposed to be winging its way to my hotel in the city, having been put in transit by my lover himself, whom I had asked to dig it out from an obscure drawer in our apartment during a frantic phone call that I placed to him as soon as I was more or less settled in town. Whether it really would reach me before I was scheduled to board my plane the next day seemed disconcertingly questionable, and the anxiety I felt about its possibly being lost and my thus being unable to reenter the United States for some time to come momentarily rendered just a little too poignant the question of exactly to where my new friend and I would have repaired had I elected to take him "home" after all.

If the discomfiture I experienced during my interview on the street is thus partly traceable to the anxiety with which I both recalled and anticipated my national-border crossing, then it would appear to constitute an instance—however paltry—of a particular psychic effect much commented upon in recent theoretical work. Specifically, it would seem to comprise the disorientation characterizing the *transnational imaginary* in the era of global capitalism. This disorientation is by no means the *only* characteristic feature of the transnationalist condition, of course. Indeed, as Priscilla Wald has noted in an extremely useful review of current thought on the issue, that condition might itself newly constitute the imagination as a site of great "explanatory potential," comprising "the intersection of social practice, individual agency, and cultural definition."[3] With this observation, Wald glosses the propositions of a number of theorists who discern the possibility of subjective empowerment within the transnationalism that they may not actually name as such. Thus Gloria Anzaldúa conceives in terms of *border-living* the "joys" and the "exhilaration" that can emanate from one's ceaselessly negotiating the "shifting and multiple identity" produced in the straddling habitation of national boundaries.[4] Smadar Lavie and Ted Swedenburg extend Anzaldúa's characterization by identifying *borderzones* as "sites of creative cultural creolization, places where criss-crossed identities are forged out of the debris of corroded, formerly (would-be) homogeneous identities."[5] Homi Bhabha identifies as a powerful effect of *cultural hybridity* the establishment of a "third space," which "displaces the histories that constitute it, and sets up new structures of authority, new political initiatives," and thus "enables other positions to emerge."[6] And, in the most explicitly *transnationalist* analysis that Wald adduces in this regard, Arjun Appadurai designates as a key aspect within contemporary global culture the rise of "*the imagination as a social practice*," which he conceives as "now central to all forms of agency."[7]

Still, such enhancement of social agency is only the flip side of transnationalism's equally deleterious effect, referenced by Anzaldúa in terms of the subjective discomfort that marks life in the borderlands, where "[h]atred, anger and exploitation are the prominent features of [the] landscape" (see her preface)—where, as Norma Alarcón puts it, "formations of violence are continuously in the making,"[8] thus constituting the borders as "zones of loss, alienation, pain, death" (Lavie and Swedenburg 15). Along with a number of the commentators whose work she engages, Wald sees a particularly powerful delineation of transnationalism's negative psychic consequences in

Theresa Hak Kyung Cha's 1982 text, *Dictée*, which characterizes Korean-immigrant experience vis-à-vis the United States as an ongoing process of subjective destabilization. In a passage that Wald references, Cha details the ritual of reentry at the U.S. border, implicating her reader within the disorientation it engenders by means of her pointedly second-person narration:

You return and you are not one of them, they treat you with indifference. All the time you understand what they are saying. But the papers give you away. Every ten feet. They ask you identity. They comment upon your inability or ability to speak. Whether you are telling the truth or not about your nationality. They say you look other than you say. As if you didn't know who you were. You say who you are but you begin to doubt. They search you. They, the anonymous variety of uniforms, each division, strata, classification, any set of miscellaneous properly uni formed. They have the right, no matter what rank, however low their function they have the authority. Their authority sewn into the stitches of their costume. Every ten feet they demand to know who and what you are, who is represented.[9]

That the border crossing Cha describes here diverges significantly from what I, a native-born U.S. citizen, experienced is self-evident; it is also to some extent precisely my point, as will become clear from what follows. Yet it seems to me that the disconcertedness I suffered is of the same order as what Cha registers, however much it may differ in degree, and however much I—native-born citizen that I am—actually brought it upon myself.

For if only I had carefully read the section of the MLA convention program titled "Entry into Canada," I would have known that "[a]lthough citizens and legal residents of the United States do not need passports or visas" in order to enter Canada from the United States, "such identification is strongly preferred," and that, in any event, "[n]ative-born United States citizens should have a birth or voter's certificate that shows citizenship."[10] I might have known this already, of course, since I had been to Toronto many times before, as well as to Montreal, Vancouver, and other Canadian locales; but the fact is that my December 1997 trip comprised the first time I had ever entered Canada by air, and while I can't vouch for the typicality of my experience, I have never once been asked to produce a passport, birth certificate, or voter registration card when crossing the U.S.-Canadian border by car.

Thinking about it now, this relative ease of entry strikes me as rather surprising, since every time I have ventured to Canada and back I have manifested at least one personal trait or dispositional characteristic liable to make crossing the border less trouble-free than one would like, the potentially questionable matters ranging from my skin color to the evident racial and gender identities of my associates; and numerous stories of which I am aware testify—as does Cha's narrative—to the nastiness that can, and often does, ensue when travellers' personal profiles diverge from the norms of legible U.S. citizenship that implicitly govern the customs-inspection procedure. At the same time, however, I don't know that my experience of smooth mobility across the northern U.S. border doesn't approximate the sanctioned understanding of what that traversal is *supposed* to be like; and, in any case, I had certainly cherished such an understanding myself prior to my journey in 1997, owing largely, I think, to the mundanity that travel to Canada was taken to represent in Detroit, Michigan, where I was born and grew up. I remember quite well, for instance, a diverting experience I had during my senior year in high school, when a friend and I, on our way to some cultural event or other, were in a car heading east on the downtown stretch of Jefferson Avenue, the principal waterfront drive along the Detroit River. Momentarily befuddled by the profusion of less-than-helpful directional signs at a key intersection, my friend, who was driving, took a wrong turn that set us irrevocably on course for the tunnel connecting Detroit to Windsor, Ontario. Breezing unimpeded through the customs station on the Canadian side of the river, we drove just far enough into Windsor to negotiate an inconspicuous U-turn, which soon brought us face-to-face with the U.S. inspector on the Detroit-bound side of the roadway. Needless to say, we had nothing to declare but our shared embarrassment, and when she was asked by the officer how long we had been in Canada, my friend said, as nonchalantly as she could, "Oh, about ten minutes"—just long enough, undoubtedly, to have picked up some confection unavailable in the States or a pack of Export A cigarettes, activities not unpursued among adolescent would-be sophisticates living in Detroit during the 1970s. That we did not engage in such consumer exchange is to some degree part of my point, however, since while our visit might have been somewhat briefer than most, it didn't seem to evoke suspicion in the official who interviewed us, to whom—as to anyone living in the region—aimless recreational cruising by Detroiters amid the sedate greenery of Windsor's riverfront neighborhoods was a thoroughly unremarkable occurrence, even when it entailed the meanderings of a white female teenaged motorist in the company of her effeminate black male classmate.

Thus, against all reason—and contrary to what I had been taught to expect in any number of other contexts—I had come to see myself as having an unproblematic claim at least to the title of U.S. citizenship, if not to all its perks and benefits, at most any point along the border with Canada—a typical condition of profound U.S.-nationalist myopia from which I was not adequately jolted until my experience in Toronto in December 1997. And yet, once that jolt took place, I immediately recurred to my default mode for negotiating the verge of subjective illegitimacy on which all nonnormative citizens are aware that we perenially teeter. Like fellow African-American members of the professional-managerial class who refuse to circulate in public attired in anything but impeccable full-corporate regalia lest they be mistaken for service staff, I eagerly asserted the official-business character of my Toronto visit, hopeful that this particular cultural-capitalist chit would win me standing in the eyes of the Canadian customs official.

Whether it worked I can't really say, and is pretty much beside the point in any case, since though I succeeded in gaining entry to Canada, I still had to contend with the problem of returning to the United States—not to mention the sense of subjective assault that I would experience until I had my papers in hand. This sense seems clearly to have informed my actions in my encounter with the man on Church Street, during which I believe I felt as much challenged in my social legitimacy as solicited in my sexual subjecthood. What on earth else could explain the idiocy whereby, in response to his asking me with whom I was in town, I said that I was there for a convention? as though the MLA itself comprised nothing other than the few thousand close friends with whom I go on annual holiday—a collection of acquaintances really too horrific to contemplate, members of the association now reading these words excepted, of course. Which is to suggest that my reaction to this man's solicitation implicated factors extending well beyond our encounter per se, bearing on matters of self and citizenship with a fully international significance.

International Trade

Given the grandness of the foregoing claim, I should elaborate the principle by which my anecdotal experiences in Toronto can be made to speak to properly sociopolitical matters at all, thereby illuminating as well one of the social elements most centrally at issue in my analysis. Leaving aside for the moment the question of exactly how the two episodes I have narrated are related to each other, it seems clear enough that my reactions within them—in addition to representing a bizarre conflation of the demands of the state and the pressures of interpersonal socialization–implicated an *anxiety* that functioned as their animating principle. Indeed, we could say that this anxiety constituted not only the force that impelled but also the *tone* that marked my invocation of my professional status, by which I responded to queries put to me in both my encounters. Cast this way, that anxiety may at first glance seem to represent only my own quirkily personal reaction to what could fairly be described as minimally stressful situations, relatively speaking. At the same time, however, Raymond Williams has cogently suggested that affective modes that may initially register as "private, idiosyncratic, and even isolating" can actually constitute experiences of profound *social* import—*structures of feeling* by which we negotiate situations and relationships in which we are immediately present, and that, because they are still in process, can ever be only partially accessible to analysis.[11]

The inevitable partialness of such analysis does not, however, render it useless or unimportant. Indeed, it is arguably only by identifying structures of feeling in their emergent manifestations—which, as Williams is careful to point out, already represent their formalization in social institutions distinct from the flux of present experience—that I can pursue the investigation into my own motives, rationales, and actions that I am taking up here. The account that I offer will necessarily be speculative, my being no more able than any "outside" party to apprehend fully the various affective elements in these exchanges, owing to their being not somehow "unconscious" but, as Williams insists, *embryonic* with respect to discernible and articulate forms (131). And if I can get at these elements only obliquely, by examining the salient expressions through which they are indicated but to which they are not reducible, this fact merely underscores the importance of *interpretation* in our critical approach to structures of feeling, suggesting how crucial is the need for readings that are *strong* in the sense of both well substantiated and consciously motivated. Such readings are valuable precisely because the structures of feeling they may help us identify can in turn indicate how *other* social structurations materially affect our daily lives.

In the instances at issue here, it would seem that the anxiety I manifested—oriented as it evidently was toward the test of social legitimacy represented in the customs interview—was a reaction specifically to the prospect of *denial* inherent within the inspection procedure. To the extent that the fundamental thwarting of will that denial connotes is generally experienced as the negation of agential subjectivity, anxiety regarding it constitutes not my own personal idiosyncrasy but rather a properly social disposition. Further, to the degree that such negation is the preeminent means by which we register the operation of *power* in our daily lives—notwithstanding the Foucauldian argument citing the pervasive impact of far more subtle disciplinary practices—then power itself would appear to be the factor of social structuration whose analysis is most compellingly demanded by my Toronto experiences.

At the same time, of course, there are various types of power, and while it seems to me that the type that was operative in my interaction on Church Street is fully as influential within daily life as that exercised by the state, which was operative in my customs interview, we cannot hope to gauge its significance without first apprehending its particular import and its specific modalities. In the interest of this latter objective, let me clarify a point registered above—that, far from obviating my usual worry about whether my partner in a flirtation is sexually attracted to me, the terms by which my interlocutor on Church Street indicated that he was willing to pursue a sexual encounter actually exacerbated my anxiety in this regard. It is clear enough, I think, why I discerned a sexual offer in his suggestion that he accompany me "home." Certainly, I might have alternatively understood him as indicating merely his need for shelter during the night, given that he had been evicted from his own place of lodging. His proposing the move immediately upon learning that my boyfriend was not with me, however, evoked the distinct possibility of our sharing such intimacy as conventionally obtains in the relation between lovers—an interpretation whose plausibility was heightened by the relatively precipitate evolution of his other recent liaison, as he described it to me. But while sex thus seemed very likely to be on the agenda, there is no forgetting that his intimation along these lines did not emerge spontaneously; rather it followed close on the heels of his asking whether I could provide him with cash, and he gave little reason to believe that my having "taken him home" in and of itself would have nullified his desires in this vein. It is this latter fact that founded my continued anxiety regarding his attraction to me, since it placed me in a most unsettling situation with respect to the highly charged category of homosexual *trade*. While in the practical idiom *trade* is a notoriously flexible—and thus, paradoxically, a remarkably useful—designation, the core sense of the term that I am invoking here is economically summed up in the classic Stonewall-era guide to gay male lingo, *The Queens' Vernacular*, according to which it denotes most basically a "nonreciprocal sex partner."[12] This characterization vividly highlights the crisis of confidence one potentially faces when confronted with trade in the sexual arena, since a partner's nonreciprocity would suggest that, whatever the terms of his gratification in the encounter, they very likely *do not* derive from his sexual attraction to one's own physical person. In the instance I have detailed here, it was clear from the outset that the primary terms of my partner's gratification derived from any monetary advantage he might have gained; while this didn't *preclude* the possibility of his actually being sexually interested in me, to boot, it absolutely did make it impossible to resolve the question to the degree required for my satisfaction.

And yet, there is more: for if, as I say, this situation was unsettling with respect to my confidence, it was nearly as much so in regard to my sense of self, because one's position relative to the category of trade can be so fully determined by seemingly innate aspects of one's being as to appear immutably fixed for one's lifetime, thus approximating the function—if not the status—of identity as such. Trade's definitional capacity along these lines—which is quite great, regardless of whether the term is ever explicitly invoked—derives from the flexibility that I have suggested it manifests, which both renders it well-nigh ubiquitous in gay male sexual culture and substantially mitigates the ego-deflating potential I have ascribed to it, so that it is actually a much more intriguing and alluring object for many men than might seem logical on first consideration. What makes dealing in trade potentially worth the maddening anxiety it can clearly engender is precisely that the nonreciprocity it entails need not register in the context of frank sexual activity at all. It might, on the contrary, characterize merely one's demeanor within the sexual *pursuit*, especially when the object of interest *really isn't* one's physical person per se but rather an aspect of that person abstracted from oneself and revered as a *fetish* by the pursuing party. In this case, the actual sexual consummation of the pursuit might register for all concerned as a fully reciprocal encounter, with each party deriving his pleasure and gratification from his experience of the other's body as related in a particular way to the fetish attribute, however extensive and abiding the fetish bearer's nonreciprocity might have been during the preliminary pursuit. Obviously, of course, actual sexual nonreciprocity can itself function as such a fetish object for certain active dealers in trade, for whom the nonaffirmation of their own physical attractiveness is a source not—or not merely—of anxiety but of sexual pleasure.

For one not so disposed, however, locating the fetish object in an aspect of a partner's physical person rather than in his sexual reserve maintains the possibility of the partner's registering his physical attraction to oneself through his active reciprocity in the sexual encounter, even while it preserves for the fetish bearer what is always the province of trade—to wit, the sense of *power* that derives from being the object of pursuit and the euphoric delirium that sense can entail.

I doubtless need not belabor the point that racial identity can serve as a prime fetish object in trade so construed, with nonwhite men frequently thus functioning as trade—and thereby enjoying the power that function connotes—in widely varying types of encounters with white men. Of course, white men can function in precisely the same capacity for men of color, too, though in that case the power with which trade is imbued would seem to register as less highly charged than it does when it attaches to a man of color, since it coincides with the very normativity that characterizes whiteness and confers it with its social supremacy within Western culture. To the degree that, conversely, a nonwhite man's function as trade extends from the fact of his social minority status—which simultaneously pervades his consciousness and thoroughly conditions his relations with white men under all circumstances—it both counters the lack of social power that minority status entails and extensively informs the sense of self entertained by a man of color who circulates not only among white gay men (when he is conceived in that context as an object of sexual interest at all, which is very frequently not the case), but within any gay male cohort socialized in the intricacies of Western race relations.[13]

This is not to deny that the fetishization underlying nonwhite men's status as trade can entail an objectification that is stultifying rather than empowering; it is merely to recognize that the effects of fetishization are irreducibly ambiguous, and that the kinds of power experienced by individuals in different social situations vary widely, along with their sources.[14] My point, though, is that availability for a particularly potent mode of fetishization is part and parcel of the minority condition, however that fetishization is experienced in terms of access to power by any minority subject in a given instance. Thus, to return to my personal exploits, for me suddenly to recognize that my interlocutor in Toronto was operating as trade in relation to me was for me to feel at once divested of the power that trade status entails, and stripped of the fetish function that, for better or worse, generally conditions my sense of who I am within gay male sexual culture. My response to this profoundly disorienting occurrence, as I have already indicated, was to flee the scene as fast as was feasible under the circumstances. Yet there are alternative ways of negotiating the factors of identity, the erotic attraction(s), and the relations of power that were at issue in the encounter I have described; and by considering these briefly, we may discover how that encounter implicated issues deriving well beyond the rendezvous itself.

My experience in the encounter detailed above very likely renders wholly self-explanatory the sense of recognition I felt in reading certain choice sections of Samuel Delany's 1994 novel, *The Mad Man*, to which I was referred by perspicacious associates familiar with my interest in the issues I am addressing here. Take, for instance, the passage in which the first-person protagonist—a young black gay man who is recounting for us his engagement, during the early 1980s, in what might best be characterized as extremely involved graduate research in philosophy—describes the aftermath of his sexual tryst with a homeless white member of the Guardian Angels amid the seats of a seedy midtown-Manhattan movie theater. Having just finished performing fellatio on the man, our narrator, John Marr—who has come directly to the cinema from his job as a temp worker in a corporate office—arises to be confronted by his partner's abrupt query:

"Hey, you got three dollars?" He added quickly: "This ain't a hustle, man. I ain't no hustler. I'm a Guardian Angel, and Angels don't do shit like that. But just as a friend, I mean. Since I gotta get out of here and find another movie to sleep in—you know what I mean? I just thought maybe . . ."

I did feel slightly like I was being hustled. Still, there I was, in suit and tie; and there he was, with no place to stay for the night. "If I have it in change," I told him, "it's yours."[15]

While John's rendering himself as the immediate object of an active hustle—rather than as simply the chance acquaintance of an innocent *hustler*—suggests that he is slightly disconcerted by the circumstances in which he finds himself, he faces those circumstances with somewhat greater equanimity than I evidenced on the street in Toronto, essentially acquiescing in his assignment to the socioeconomic position that his attire signals, even though it does not comport with his own sense of himself in the encounter. I would like to propose that John's relative calm in the face of potential identic disjuncture is but a small indication of his willingness actually to *mobilize* identity in relation to power for the sake of maximally intense erotic effect. A good number of the novel's many examples in this vein entail the standard deployment of black men's fetish status in the function of trade, and so nicely illustrate the point I make above regarding the potential centrality of that status within black gay men's sense of self. For instance, having become acquainted—in the balcony of a *different* midtown movie theater—with an approximately thirty-year-old white carpenter from New Jersey named Dave who, by his own account, "like[s] sucking black dick more than just about anything in the world!" (140), John escorts the man on his first excursion to Wet Night, the recurrent golden shower party held once monthly at the legendary Mineshaft bar and sex club, in the meat-packing district on the western edge of Greenwich Village. Once they get there, accompanied by John's West Indian friend Pheldon and joined later by an anonymous third black man whom they don't know, a small private orgy ensues during which the three black men alternately urinate on and are fellated by Dave, all four of them eventually driven to orgasmic climax on the power of their collectively deployed racial fetishization. Not only is the commonality of the sexual pleasure achieved through this deployment emphatically invoked by the anonymous black man as he turns to leave the others—"Ain't nothin' like peein' on a white boy," he declares, "It just makes *everybody* feel good, don't it?" (152)—but the experience actually solidifies the relationship between John and Pheldon, who before this have never engaged in sexual activity together. Worrying over breakfast the next morning that this novel development might negatively affect their friendship, Pheldon confesses to John that, while as an acknowledged "snow queen" he has an abiding predilection for white men, so that "most of my affections go toward the Daves of this world . . . [,] the fact is, John, I don't *have* a lot of black, gay, men friends. You mean a lot to me." "He was cute as a button," John replies, adding, "I kind of got off, sharing him with you. . . ." Surprised, Pheldon exclaims, "You did?" and then offers the final observation, "You know, we really *are* friends, aren't we?" (155, ellipsis added). Thus the black men's highly motivated, eroticized engagement with the fact of their fetish status actually affirms their sense of self not only as individuals but as a social entity rendered ever more cohesive through its developing consciousness regarding its minority condition.[16]

This process seems not to go forward along normal lines, however, when at an earlier—and pivotal—point in the novel John is confronted by a mode of nonnormativity whose significance registers as greater than his own. Intent on solving the mystery surrounding the murder of the young Korean-American philosophic prodigy Timothy Hasler—with whose intellectual legacy John and his faculty adviser, Irving Mossman, are both obsessed—John embarks on an attempt to recreate the unconventional gay sex life that Mossman, relying on fragmentary biographical materials, has deduced that Hasler led. Thus impelled to scour Riverside Park in search of the disheveled, unwashed, and decrepit homeless men whom he believes Hasler had favored, John forwards his quest by offering to suck the dick of just about every displaced man he discovers lounging on a park bench. Undeterred by either the hostility he occasionally meets with or the demands for money up front that he receives from the trade he encounters, he finally finds a man who takes him up on his suggestion. Not gay-identified himself—though he is eager to tell his new African-American acquaintance of his fetishistic enthusiasm for black women—this white man eagerly introduces John to a wide array of arcane sexual practices that they both find immensely pleasurable; but these activities are less noteworthy for my purposes here than the terms by which the men designate themselves for each other at the start of their relationship. Having insisted to John, "I ain't no faggot," the homeless man goes on to say, "But I always had me a good imagination. So if a cocksucker don't mind me doin' a little thinkin', a little imaginin', I sure don't mind no cocksucker . . . nursin' on my fuckin' peter" (30–31). Taking in both this assertion and the man's characterization of himself as generally no better than "dog shit," John laughs and then asks, "What's your name?"

> *"What's yours?"*
>
> *"Might as well call me 'cocksucker.' . . . Since that's what I do. And yourself?"*
>
> *"Well, I'll tell you, . . . [y]ou call me a piece o' shit, and you'll be callin' me a lot better'n what most people done called me most of my life." (31)*

With mutual obligingness, the two men immediately begin addressing each other as "cocksucker" and "Piece of Shit," a practice that they carry on through the entirety of the long episode, and that suggests a rather different significance for this encounter than for the golden shower episode described above.

If the black men's function as the dispensing participants in the aforementioned round of water sports figures both their motivated occupation of their fetishized status and their deployment of it as a means to power rather than degradation, John's assumption of the title "cocksucker" here may serve a similar function (though, it would seem, to a less dramatic degree) with respect to his homosexual identification, but his use of the phrase "Piece of Shit" as the designation for his acquaintance accomplishes something altogether different. While in this narrative sequence John appears paradoxically as the socially normative subject in comparison to his friend, the friend himself appears as the social effluvium against which normativity is defined and measured; is *named* as such in the scatological designation by which he invites John to address him; and is *embraced* as such by John both in the remarkably intimate instance of their extended sexual liaison and in John's occasional reference to the man as not simply "Piece of Shit" but "*my* Piece of Shit" (e.g., 51; emphasis added). This latter action on John's part seems to me to constitute a highly distinctive mode of negotiating the complex dynamics of power, identity, and erotic investment that were crucially at work in my own encounter with trade on the street in Toronto. I am interested in this mode not because I want to propose it as some better alternative model that I ought to have followed in my personal experience, as awestruck by it as I must admit myself to be. Rather, I am interested in it because, in the terms it so explicitly engages and deploys, it seems clearly to indicate the ultimate meaning of the course I did pursue in my encounter. Specifically, John's relationship with "his" Piece of Shit figures an accepting engagement with the literally *abject* that suggests to me the latter's divergent significance in my Church Street incident.[17] While I obviously was preoccupied with my potentially being cast as the *sexually* abject within that episode, the category bears an undeniable *sociopolitical* significance as well. That the two levels of meaning were extensively intertwined in that instance not only accounts somewhat for my confusion during the meeting, it also helps explain how the category was mobilized so as to have the effect that it finally did.

At Home in the World

The fact that my encounter on Church Street was far removed from the border crossing at which I felt my first twinge of transnationalist anxiety does not at all mean that it did not implicate a transnational experience, founded in the very terms by which my acquaintance boldly forwarded our exchange. Specifically, by unhesitatingly detailing for me the vicissitudes in his liaison with his erstwhile companion and presumptuously asking after my own boyfriend, the man assimilated us both to a culture of male homoerotic relations in which such enunciations effectively serve as a lingua franca bridging all manner of national-cultural difference. Thus we might be said to have constituted our own little transnational formation, the two of us functioning as elements in what could (given Appadurai's theorizations in this vein) be called a multinational *ethnoscape* whose otherwise disparate members share common principles of sexual conduct and thus are enabled to negotiate our chance encounters in relatively expedient terms.[18] I daresay I am well aware of what those terms are, and yet quite clearly was already eschewing them at a fairly early point in our conversation.

Let us remember, after all, that when the man asked me with whom I was in Toronto—the solicitational import of which query was not lost on me—I told him I was in town for a convention. I have already suggested that the anxiety about social status arguably informing this overcompensatingly professionalist response is endemic among classes of U.S. citizens who feel compromised as civil subjects owing to the ways that aspects of their social identities are apprehended in the public sphere. To personalize the terms in which Judy Grahn characterized this situation, while the question of to whom I am married is of no great consequence for my social standing (which is not to say that it is not important at all or that it is any less irritating to me when it is posed), I tacitly vowed long ago that there would always be a valid answer forthcoming when anyone asked about me, "What does she do?"—and I doubt very much that I am alone in this among U.S. professionals of any number of colors. At the same time, though, it is quite clear that the import of my interview on the street differed significantly from what obtains at the customs inspection, which by definition incorporates an official challenge to subjective legitimacy. Consequently, my responding to the man's query with an effective assertion of my professional status would seem to represent a curious misapplication of a strategy for meeting the demands of state power in a context where such power was not evidently in play.

Of course, as I have strived to demonstrate in the preceding section of this essay, a certain other type of power most definitely *was* at issue in my sidewalk encounter, the effects of this fact registering for me at the outset of the meeting in a way recognizable from the foregoing observations. After all, from the moment I conceived my solicitor as an object of sexual desire—which is to say, from the moment I saw him—our interview bore the potential for eventuating, from my perspective, in exactly the thwarting of will through which I have suggested we become cognizant of power as such. On this view, the power at stake would manifest specifically in terms of access to sexual liaison, even as, from the standpoint my partner effectively claimed with his request for money, it manifested in terms of access to cash. That these two sets of terms did not function independent of each other as our interaction progressed is already quite clear, since my interlocutor ultimately indicated his full willingness actually to exchange sex for material gain. Even prior to consolidating the disparate stakes of our engagement by tendering this offer, though, the man pressed our acquaintance by maneuvering fluidly between the terms of sex and money in play from the beginning. Noting how I balked at his request for cash, the man alternatively forwarded the sexual dimension of our conversation through his pointed query regarding who was accompanying me in Toronto. With the sexual stakes of the exchange thus raised to prominence—but the possibility of confidence-quelling denial along these lines in no way diminished, for all that heightening—my misapprehending response that I was in town for a professional convention worked to offset the abiding risk of sexual refusal by diverting the conversation toward the entirely new terms of *social status*, related to and yet not identical with the terms of sexual access and, especially, financial disposition that were already operative. While the effects of this particular gambit were short-lived, at best—my interlocutor corrected my misapprehension and more explicitly reasserted the sexual import of his query—they anticipated and largely coincided with those deriving from my ultimate move in the encounter.

For by finally giving the man money—however minimal a sum—and immediately quitting his company, I essentially constituted him as a panhandler after all, despite his initial protestations to the contrary. In so doing, I simultaneously foreclosed the possibility of our sexual encounter, imbued as it was with as much risk as excitement, and underscored the extent to which, for all our shared sexual ethic and potential mutual erotic attraction, he and I radically diverged in terms of both our current financial situations and our social statuses. To what end I accomplished this seems completely uncertain, however, since while social status might have figured fetishistically in the pleasure deriving from any sexual encounter we pursued, it evidently was not one of the clear stakes in our negotiation, and indeed it appears quite likely that my acquaintance didn't care about it one whit.

Moreover, while my similar assertion of my social position at the Canadian customs desk may appear somewhat more intelligible—in that it really *is* a mode of social legitimacy for which the customs personnel are seeking when they scrutinize one at the national border—it actually was only slightly more appropriate there than in the context of my sidewalk solicitation. After all, if testimony as to one's professional position and consequent social status can help validate one's purpose in traveling to a given country, it goes no distance whatsoever in verifying one's official citizenship—except perhaps in the realm of an *imaginary* that is actually not transnational at all.

Tracing the effects of a particular fantasy of the American Dream that has solidified its purchase on the collective national psyche since the earliest days of the first Reagan administration, Lauren Berlant has suggestively argued that this fantasy identifies *citizenship* not with a recognized set of rights and liberties whose significance is continually reevaluated and adjusted through the operations of a properly political public sphere but, rather, with the achievement of a *social mobility* in the shadow of whose growing importance persistent systemic inequalities and impediments to popular political power become effectively obscured. In other words, this increasingly officialized fantasy authorizes the conceptualization of socioeconomic status

as the substance of U.S. citizenship itself.[19] In this case, the bourgeois U.S. national's anxious assertion of his or her socioeconomic status in *whatever* context might be read as an insecurely aggressive grasping at the prize of a citizenship whose value is implicitly understood to be great even as its meaning inexorably recedes from view. Nor is this activity without collateral social effect, as is indicated by my dealings with the man on Church Street. For if in that encounter my ultimate evocation of my socioeconomic status marked as the actual object of my worry legitimate U.S. citizenship, then by emphatically situating the man in a position of socioeconomic inferiority I really was doing nothing less than constituting him as the abject of my own civil subjecthood in a nation that we didn't even inhabit at the moment.

Thus, while it might be said that the subjective disorientation I suffered during my sojourn in Canada represented my personal reckoning with the psychic dimensions of transnationalism, it can in no way be denied that, in this instance, the transnationalist engagement itself was ineluctably forwarded along specifically U.S.-nationalist lines. That such a suspicious deployment can be effected by the state in the interest of properly political ends has been aptly demonstrated by Kandice Chuh, in an incisively cautionary analysis focused on the U.S. government's internment of Japanese Americans during World War II.[20] The foregoing consideration would seem to locate a similar capacity in the psychic imaginary, which even in its most individuated and privatized instantiations might negotiate the terms of transnationalism so as to solidify the identification of the individual "citizen" with the national entity whose hegemony transnationalism itself has been understood to challenge. All of which reminds us of what we already know—that state-ideological functions can never be conceived apart from the citizen-subjects whose activities and consciousness they call into being, which themselves certainly have not yet been unmoored from the imperatives of modern state-nationalism. In that case—and at this point—with respect to the United States, the most effective instances of transnational analysis may very likely be those that begin at home.

1998–99

Notes

1. Titled "Gay Identities, Personal Privacy, and Relations of Public Exchange," the paper was presented as part of the session "Embattled Masculinities in Popular Culture," arranged by the Division on Popular Culture, José Esteban Muñoz, presiding, Modern Language Association convention, Toronto, Ontario, Canada, 29 December 1997.

The incident in question is briefly addressed in the similarly titled article "Gay Male Identities, Personal Privacy, and Relations of Public Exchange: Notes on Directions for Queer Critique," which appears in this volume; and I interrogate it extensively in the book *Invasions of Privacy: Identity and Exchange in the Contest of Everyday Life,* forthcoming from New York University Press.

2. Judy Grahn, "A Woman Is Talking to Death" (1973), in *The Work of a Common Woman: The Collected Poetry of Judy Grahn, 1964–1977* (1978; New York: St. Martin's, 1980; reprint Freedom, Calif.: The Crossing Press) 117.

3. Priscilla Wald, "Minefields and Meeting Grounds: Transnational Analyses and American Studies," *American Literary History* 10.1 (Spring 1998): 210.

4. Gloria Anzaldúa, "Preface," *Borderlands: The New Mestiza* (San Francisco: Aunt Lute, 1987).

5. Smadar Lavie and Ted Swedenburg, "Introduction: Displacement, Diaspora, and Geographies of Identity," *Displacement, Diaspora, and Geographies of Identity,* ed. Lavie and Swedenburg (Durham, N.C.: Duke University Press, 1996) 15.

6. Homi Bhabha, "The Third Space," interview conducted by Jonathan Rutherford, in Rutherford, ed., *Identity: Community, Culture, Difference* (London: Lawrence and Wishart, 1990) 211.

7. Arjun Appadurai, "Disjuncture and Difference in the Global Cultural Economy," chapter 2 of *Modernity at Large: Cultural Dimensions of Globalization*, Public Worlds, vol. 1 (Minneapolis: University of Minnesota Press, 1996) 27–47; 31 for the pertinent passage, emphasis in the original.

8. Norma Alarcón, "Anzaldúa's *Frontera:* Inscribing Gynetics," in Lavie and Swedenburg, 44.

9. Theresa Hak Kyung Cha, *Dictée* (1982; Berkeley, Calif.: Third Woman Press, 1995) 56–57.

For Wald's assessment of Cha's significance, see Wald, "Minefields and Meeting Grounds," 214.

10. "About the MLA Convention," *PMLA* 112.6 (November 1997; Convention Program Issue): 1208.

11. Raymond Williams, "Structures of Feeling," *Marxism and Literature*, Marxist Introductions (Oxford: Oxford University Press, 1977) 132.

12. Bruce Rodgers, *The Queens' Vernacular: A Gay Lexicon* (San Francisco: Straight Arrow Books, 1972) 199–200.

13. On, for example, black gay men's implication in the erotic fetishization of black male physicality, see Darieck Scott, "Jungle Fever? Black Gay Identity Politics, White Dick, and the Utopian Bedroom," *GLQ: A Journal of Lesbian and Gay Studies* 1.3 (1994): 299–321.

14. For what is by now the classic critical engagement with the ambiguous significances of racial fetishism for black men in the Western context, see Kobena Mercer, "Reading Racial Fetishism," *Welcome to the Jungle: New Positions in Black Cultural Studies* (New York: Routledge, 1994) 171–219.

15. Samuel R. Delany, *The Mad Man* (1994; New York: Rhinoceros, 1996) 136, ellipsis in original.

16. One of our most cannily self-aware commentators on sexuality, Delany had, by the time he published *The Mad Man*, already documented his own fetishistic interest—focused on men's work-worn, broad-fingered, nail-bitten hands—in his 1988 memoir, *The Motion of Light in Water* (New York: Plume, 1989); see, for example pages 10, 26, 36, 290. Moreover, pertinent for the discussion that follows, the autobiographical narrative traces Delany's own erotic engagements with various exemplars of social abjection, prominent among them Bob, the young white drifter, hustler, and ex-convict with whom Delany and poet Marilyn Hacker, to whom Delany was then married, maintained an extensive ménage through the first half of 1965; see pp. 252–87. For a fuller account of Delany's biography during this period, see the unexpurgated edition of the memoir (New York: Richard Kasak, 1993).

17. More recent work by Delany himself offers an extremely useful gloss on the sorts of encounters detailed both in *The Mad Man* and in Delany's autobiographical writing, conceptualizing them as instances of powerful cross-class "contact" with far-reaching significance within U.S. culture and society. See Samuel R. Delany, *Times Square Red, Times Square Blue: An Inquiry into Some Modes of Urban Sociality*, Sexual Cultures (New York: New York University Press, 1999); most pertinent in this vein is the extended second section of the book, ". . . Three, Two, One, Contact: Times Square Red, 1997."

Mikko Tuhkanen offers an analysis of Delany's *The Mad Man* that resonates powerfully with what I present here, even as it diverges from my argument in significant—and useful—ways. His observations appear in the paper "Homoness/Homelessness: Sexuality and Community in Samuel R. Delany's *The Mad Man*," which was delivered at the seminar "Homo Academicus: Gay, Lesbian, and Queer Research," University of Turku, Finland, 9–10 October 1998.

18. Appadurai, *Modernity at Large,* 33–34; see also his chapter 3, "Global Ethnoscapes: Notes and Queries for a Transnational Anthropology," 48–65.

19. See Lauren Berlant, *The Queen of America Goes to Washington City: Essays on Sex and Citizenship*, Series Q (Durham, N.C.: Duke University Press, 1997), especially the Introduction, "The Intimate Public Sphere," 1–24.

It occurs to me that the phenomenon that Berlant cites might constitute an inevitable development in the significance of "possessive individualism" within the West during the twentieth century, stemming from what C. B. Macpherson has identified as the effective crisis in social equality brought about by the increases in class stratification, class cohesiveness, and class consciousness attending the rise of industrialization from the late nineteenth century on. See Macpherson, *The Political Theory of Possessive Individualism: Hobbes to Locke* (Oxford: Oxford University Press, 1962), especially pp. 271–77.

20. Kandice Chuh, "Transnationalism and Its Pasts," *Public Culture* 9.1 (Fall 1996): 93–112.

Afterword

In the week immediately following President Clinton's August 17, 1998, address—far too soon to have accounted for the speech in its pages—the *New Yorker* magazine published a special issue devoted to the topic of private lives (*Private Lives, The New Yorker* 24 and 31 August 1998). Featured in that issue's edition of the regular "Talk of the Town" section was an entry facetiously logged under the "Silver Lining Dept.," the ostensible object of which was to consider the reasons for Hillary Rodham Clinton's advance in the popularity polls during the months when it was becoming increasingly clear that the president had had *some* sort of "inappropriate" relationship with Monica Lewinsky in the early part of the decade. Remarking especially the groundswell of support for Mrs. Clinton among women who identified as "nonfeminists," item author Jane Mayer cited Democratic pollster Celinda Lake as asserting that such women felt more identified with the First Lady at that point than they had during the preceding five and a half years, since she now seemed more like "most women," who "don't have power and control over the men in their lives" (50).

The implicit judgment that Mrs. Clinton was suddenly deprived of the overweening influence she had exerted over her husband during the earlier portion of his administration begs a number of questions, among them whether such "control" had ever actually been at stake in the Clintons' relationship in the first place or whether, on the contrary, either of them could really have cared less with whom the other had sex, where, and how often. More than this, though, the assessment—however comforting it might have been at the time to any number of constituencies—is grounded in the faulty assumption that any of us can reliably *determine* the character of other people's interpersonal relationship based on evidence we discern from its "public" aspect, which is to say, any aspect of it made manifest to an outside party. Indeed, author Mayer was careful to debunk precisely this notion later in the piece, plainly declaring that "image and reality are rarely identical in politics," and proposing that Mrs. Clinton "has probably seldom had more power than she has right now," since she "is one of the very few people who can talk to the President about his legal troubles without risking having to tell a grand jury about it" (50–51).

Be that as it might, the insight that Mayer registered regarding the disjuncture between "image and reality"—and I daresay we would be hard pressed to identify a realm even *beyond* national politics where this disjuncture does not obtain—seems to have dawned on her too late to benefit the analysis she offered in the immediately preceding paragraph, which limned a cognate dissonance to that between appearance and fact, designated, as we might expect, as the difference between "public" and "private." Acknowledging "Mrs. Clinton's apparent composure in recent months" and the First Couple's evident joint determination to "be . . . as affectionate as ever with each other in public," Mayer divulged that, nevertheless, "in private, some recent visitors have detected strain. A White House dinner last month ended with the men and women separating into two casual groups, almost, according to one guest, 'as if Clinton couldn't wait to get away and be with the guys'" (50). While at first glance operating as it seems to have been engineered to do—that is, showing up the irreducible difference between presentational front and hidden experience—this passage actually incorporates the faulty logic that the piece overall is meant to expose, grounding the putative reliability of its claims in the mere fact that they derived in a context blithely and unquestioningly identified as "private."

It is an open question, however, to what degree a social event, of whatever size, held at the White House—or at whatever venue—actually constitutes a "private" realm along the lines of what Mayer suggests, inasmuch as stratagems of self-presentation are extensively at work in such settings so as potentially to make for rather different impressions of those in attendance than would be registered even in a group that varied only in composition, let alone under more recognizably "intimate" circumstances. In other words—to borrow a concept from Nancy Franklin, author of the opening "Comment" in the *Public Lives* issue of the *New Yorker*—there is arguably as much "craft," however unconscious or unthinking, operative in face-to-face social interaction as Franklin urges should be deployed in the drafting of the confessional memoir whose overabundance at the end of the 1990s she, like so many other contemporary observers, couldn't help but note (12).

Indeed, it is precisely her faith in the "virtues of craft" that impels Franklin not to decry but, rather, to champion the writing of memoir, properly pursued; after all, she points out, those virtues amount to "communicative tools in their own right," however much this fact may go unrecognized in favor of "the fallacy that the unvarnished truth is the whole truth and the only truth. (It is really just another way of approximating truth.)" Leaving aside the inevitable knotty question as to what constitutes the mode of truth to which Franklin refers, I would like to extend her suggestion that the valuable education in the ways of the world that memoiristic narrative offers derives from its capacity to "ignit[e] our imagination"(12).

There is much to be said for imagination, after all, even beyond the pleasure it affords when we use it, say, to conjure what *really* goes on in the First Couple's bedchamber; or even aside from the guidelines for living that Franklin suggests it can provide when we conscientiously bring it to bear on our experience of biographical vignette.

While these rewards are not to be sneezed at, they do not necessarily entail the properly analytical mode of engagement that I have strived to pursue in the foregoing pages, in which I would argue imagination must also play a primary role. The object in this case is not to get at the "truth" of the events—and particularly the memoiristic ones—under critical review, which Franklin cautions us would be a futile effort, regardless. Rather, it is to determine the meaning of the *forms* in and through which those events develop—a whole other order of truth, I believe, than even what Franklin has in mind when she suggests that the "coat of varnish" represented in narrative "craft" "brings out the grain of the wood" by which she metaphorically references the significance of biographical experience (12). For such experience *does* comprise a truth that is accessible to our comprehension, if we consider that experience itself must necessarily issue not from the mysterious inner workings of the individual psyche who strives to call its meaning to the fore but, rather, from the *relations* through which it is lived, which themselves constitute the forms of life's events, referenced in the passage above.

One such form we have implicitly agreed to call *privacy*, and the name will do as well as any. We tell ourselves that secreted within that form lie truths we can never plumb, and this may be so. But the form itself is fully open to scrutiny, and indeed demands that we subject it to such. For its effects on individuals, on groups, and on society in general are by no means uniformly beneficial, however comforting—and even helpful—they frequently are. The truth of those effects would be one object of our examination; how we can alter them would be another. And as difficult as it undeniably is to transform those effects, those forms, those relations, we have absolutely no hope of succeeding at all if we cannot imagine how they might be different.

Bibliography

"About the MLA Convention." *PMLA* 112.6 (November 1997; Convention Program Issue): 1204–11.

Alarcón, Norma. "Anzaldúa's *Frontera:* Inscribing Gynetics." Lavie and Swedenburg 41–53.

Althusser, Louis. "Ideology and Ideological State Apparatuses (Notes towards an Investigation)." *Lenin and Philosophy and Other Essays.* Trans. Ben Brewster. New York: Monthly Review Press, 1971. 127–86.

American Heritage Dictionary of the English Language, The. Ed. William Morris. Boston: Houghton Mifflin, 1973.

Anzaldúa, Gloria. *Borderlands: The New Mestiza.* San Francisco: Aunt Lute, 1987.

Appadurai, Arjun. *Modernity at Large: Cultural Dimensions of Globalization.* Public Worlds 1. Minneapolis: University of Minnesota Press, 1996.

Austin, J. L. *How to Do Things with Words.* The William James Lectures delivered at Harvard University in 1955. Ed. J. O. Urmson and Marina Sbisà. 2nd ed. Cambridge: Harvard University Press, 1975.

Balfour, Ian. "The Playhouse of the Signifier." Penley and Willis 155–67.

Barron, James. "Street News, Sold by Poor, Falls on Hard Times Itself." *New York Times* 21 December 1994: B3.

Berlant, Lauren. *The Queen of America Goes to Washington City: Essays on Sex and Citizenship.* Series Q. Durham, N.C.: Duke University Press, 1997.

Berlant, Lauren, and Elizabeth Freeman. "Queer Nationality." Warner 193–229.

Berlant, Lauren, and Michael Warner. "Guest Column: What Does Queer Theory Teach Us about *X?*" *PMLA* 110.3 (May 1995): 343–49.

Bhabha, Homi. "The Third Space." Interview conducted by Jonathan Rutherford. *Identity: Community, Culture, Difference*. Ed. Rutherford. London: Lawrence and Wishart, 1990. 207–21.

Bowers, Attorney General of Georgia v. Hardwick et al. 478 U.S. 186–220. 1986.

Butler, Judith. *Bodies That Matter: On the Discursive Limits of "Sex."* New York: Routledge, 1993.

———. "Critically Queer." *GLQ: A Journal of Lesbian and Gay Studies* 1.1 (1993): 17–32. Also, with variations, *Bodies That Matter* 223–42.

———. "Gender Is Burning: Questions of Appropriation and Subversion." *Bodies That Matter* 121–40.

———. *Gender Trouble: Feminism and the Subversion of Identity*. New York: Routledge, 1990.

Canby, Vincent. "Aching to Be a Prima Donna, When You're a Man." *New York Times* 13 March 1991: B3.

Cha, Theresa Hak Kyung. *Dictée*. 1982. Berkeley, Calif.: Third Woman Press, 1995.

Champigneulle, Bernard. *Rodin*. Trans. and adapt. J. Maxwell Brownjohn. New York: Abrams, 1967.

Chesnutt, Charles W. *The Marrow of Tradition*. 1901. New York: Arno Press, 1969.

Chuh, Kandice. "Transnationalism and Its Pasts." *Public Culture* 9.1 (Fall 1996): 93–112.

Crimp, Douglas. "Right On, Girlfriend!" Warner 300–20.

———, ed. *AIDS: Cultural Analysis/Cultural Activism*. Special issue of *October* 43 (Winter 1987).

Delany, Samuel R. *The Mad Man*. 1994. New York: Rhinoceros, 1996.

———. *The Motion of Light in Water: Sex and Science Fiction Writing in the East Village, 1957–1965*. 1988. New York: Plume, 1989. New York: Richard Kasak, unexpurgated edition 1993.

———. *Times Square Red, Times Square Blue: An Inquiry into Some Modes of Urban Sociality*. Sexual Cultures. New York: New York University Press, 1999.

Denby, David. "Movies." *New York* 19 August 1991: 50–51.

Donohue, Timothy E. *In the Open: Diary of a Homeless Alcoholic*. Chicago: University of Chicago Press, 1996.

Doty, Alexander. "The Sissy Boy, the Fat Ladies, and the Dykes: Queerness and/as Gender in Pee-wee's World." *Camera Obscura* 25–26 (January/May 1991): 125–43.

Duesberg, Peter H. *Infectious AIDS: Have We Been Misled?* Berkeley, Calif.: North Atlantic Books, 1995.

———. *Inventing the AIDS Virus*. Washington, D.C.: Regnery, 1996.

———, ed. *AIDS: Virus- or Drug Induced?* Dordrecht; Boston: Kluwer Academic Publishers, 1996.

Easthope, Antony. *Poetry As Discourse*. New Accents. Series ed. Terence Hawkes. London and New York: Methuen, 1983.

Egan, Jennifer. "Uniforms in the Closet." *New York Times Magazine* 28 June 1998: 26+

Eighner, Lars. *American Prelude*. New York: Badboy, 1994.

———. *Bayou Boy*. New York: Badboy, 1993.

———. *B.M.O.C.* New York: Badboy, 1993.

———. *Travels with Lizbeth: Three Years on the Road and on the Streets*. New York: St. Martin's, 1993.

———. *Whispered in the Dark and Other Stories*. New York: Badboy, 1995.

Ellis, John. "Photography/Pornography/Art/Pornography," *Screen* 21.1 (Spring 1980): 81–108.

Elsen, Albert E. "When the Sculptures Were White." *Rodin Rediscovered*. Exhibition Catalogue. Ed. Elsen. Washington, D.C.: National Gallery of Art; Boston: Little, Brown/New York Graphic Society, 1981. 127–50.

Engels, Friedrich. *The Origin of the Family, Private Property, and the State*. 1884. New York: International Publishers, 1942.

Farber, Jim. "Clothes Make the Man." *Mother Jones* 16.2 (March/April 1991): 75.

Franklin, Nancy. "Comment: Show and Tell." *Private Lives* 11–12.

Freud, Sigmund. *An Outline of Psycho-Analysis*. 1940 (1938). *The Standard Edition of the Complete Psychological Works of Sigmund Freud*. Trans. James Strachey. Vol. 23. London: Hogarth, 1964. 139–207.

Freud, Sigmund. "Fetishism." 1927. *The Standard Edition.* Vol. 21. London: Hogarth, 1961. 147–57.

Froelich, Janet. "Cover Boy." *New York Times Magazine* 10 November 1996: 50–51.

Fuss, Diana. *Identification Papers.* New York: Routledge, 1995.

Gaines, Jane M. *Contested Culture: The Image, the Voice, and the Law.* Chapel Hill: University of North Carolina Press, 1991.

Geist, Sidney. *Brancusi: A Study of the Sculpture.* New York: Grossman, 1968.

Grahn, Judy. "A Woman Is Talking to Death." 1973. *The Work of a Common Woman: The Collected Poetry of Judy Grahn, 1964–1977.* 1978. New York: St. Martin's, 1980. Reprint, Freedom, Calif.: The Crossing Press. 113–31.

Green, Jesse. "Paris Has Burned." *New York Times* 18 April 1993: section 9, pp. 1, 11.

Gross, Larry. *Contested Closets: The Politics and Ethics of Outing.* Minneapolis: University of Minnesota Press, 1993.

Habermas, Jürgen. *The Structural Transformation of the Public Sphere: An Inquiry into a Category of Bourgeois Society.* Trans. Thomas Burger, with Frederick Lawrence. Studies in Contemporary German Social Thought. Cambridge: MIT Press, 1989.

Halley, Janet E. "The Status/Conduct Distinction in the 1993 Revisions to Military Anti-Gay Policy: A Legal Archaeology." *GLQ: A Journal of Lesbian and Gay Studies* 3.2–3 (1996): 159–252.

Harper, Frances Ellen Watkins. *Iola Leroy; or, Shadows Uplifted.* 1892. Intro. Hazel V. Carby. Black Women Writers. Series ed. Deborah E. McDowell. Boston: Beacon, 1987.

hooks, bell. "Is Paris Burning?" *Black Looks: Race and Representation.* Boston: South End Press, 1992. 145–56.

Howell, John. "Exits and Entrances: On Voguing." *Artforum* February 1989: 9–11.

Humphreys, Laud. *Tearoom Trade: Impersonal Sex in Public Places.* 1970. New York: Aldine, enlarged ed. 1975.

Hunter, Nan D. "Sexual Dissent and the Family." *The Nation* 253.11 (7 October 1991): 406–11.

"In His Own Words." Text of President Bill Clinton's televised statement of 17 August 1998. *New York Times* 18 August 1998: A12.

Jacobs, Sally. "News Is Uplifting for Homeless in N.Y." *Boston Globe* 7 May 1990: 1, 7.

———. "Somerville Paper Touts a Prior Claim to Street Beat." *Boston Globe* 2 July 1990: 15, 26.

Jenkins, Henry, III. "'Going Bonkers!': Children, Play and Pee-wee." Penley and Willis 169–92.

Klawans, Stewart. Review of *Paris Is Burning*. *The Nation* 252.15 (22 April 1991): 535–36.

Kluge, Alexander. *Alexander Kluge: Theoretical Writings, Stories, and an Interview*. Ed. Stuart Liebman. Special issue of *October* 46 (Fall 1988).

———. "Begriff des Zuschauers." *Bestandsaufnahme: Utopie Film: Zwanzig Jahre neuer deutscher Film/Mitte 1983*. Frankfurt am Main: Zweitausendeins, 1983. 94–95.

———. "On Film and the Public Sphere." Trans. Thomas Y. Levin and Miriam B. Hansen. *New German Critique* 24–25 (Fall/Winter 1981–82): 206–20.

LaFontaine, David, and Patrick Ward. "Why our future is in the GOP." *Gay Community News* 18.28 (4–10 February 1991): 5.

Lavie, Smadar, and Ted Swedenburg, eds. *Displacement, Diaspora, and Geographies of Identity*. Durham, N.C.: Duke University Press, 1996.

Leone, Matthew. "Bye Bye *Street News*?" *Columbia Journalism Review* May/June 1995: 22.

McAllister, Shawn. "Street News May Fold." *Editor and Publisher* 25 February 1995: 16–17.

McAuley, Christine. "Liza Minelli Sells Well, Particularly in Subway Trains." *Wall Street Journal* 27 February 1990: A1, A12.

Macpherson, C. B. *The Political Theory of Possessive Individualism: Hobbes to Locke*. Oxford: Oxford University Press, 1962.

Mayer, Jane. "Silver Lining Dept." Item in "Talk of the Town." *Private Lives*, 50–51.

Mercer, Kobena. "Reading Racial Fetishism." *Welcome to the Jungle: New Positions in Black Cultural Studies*. New York: Routledge, 1994. 171–219.

Miller, D. A. "Secret Subjects, Open Secrets." *The Novel and the Police*. Berkeley: University of California Press, 1988. 192–220.

Mohr, Richard D. *Gays/Justice: A Study of Ethics, Society, and Law*. New York: Columbia University Press, 1988.

Muñoz, José Esteban. "Famous and Dandy Like B. 'n' Andy: Race, Pop, and Basquiat." *Pop Out: Queer Warhol*. Ed. Jennifer Doyle, Jonathan Flatley, and Muñoz. Series Q. Durham, N.C.: Duke University Press, 1996. 144–79.

———. "'The White to Be Angry': Vaginal Davis's Terrorist Drag." *Queer Transexions of Race, Nation, and Gender*. Ed. Phillip Brian Harper, Anne McClintock, Muñoz, and Trish Rosen. Special double issue of *Social Text* 52/53 (15.3–4; Fall/Winter 1997): 80–103.

Muther, Christopher. "2 Men Sue Crane Beach Trustees after Sex Arrest." *Bay Windows* (Boston) 15 July 1993: 3, 10.

Navarre, Max. "Fighting the Victim Label." Crimp, *AIDS* 143–46.

Negt, Oskar, and Alexander Kluge. *Public Sphere and Experience: Toward an Analysis of the Bourgeois and Proletarian Public Sphere*. Trans. Peter Labanyi, Jamie Owen Daniel, and Assenka Oksiloff. Theory and History of Literature 85. Minneapolis: University of Minnesota Press, 1993.

New German Critique 49 (Winter 1990), special issue on Alexander Kluge.

Pateman, Carole. "Feminist Critiques of the Public/Private Dichotomy." *The Disorder of Women: Democracy, Feminism and Political Theory*. Stanford: Stanford University Press, 1989. 118–40.

Penley, Constance, and Sharon Willis, eds. *Male Trouble*, special issue of *Camera Obscura* 17 (May 1988).

Penley, Constance. "The Cabinet of Dr. Pee-wee: Consumerism and Sexual Terror." Penley and Willis 133–53.

Private Lives. Special issue of the *New Yorker* 24 and 31 August 1998.

Pronger, Brian. *The Arena of Masculinity: Sports, Homosexuality, and the Meaning of Sex*. New York: St. Martin's, 1990.

"PWA Coalition Portfolio." Crimp, *AIDS* 147–68.

Reid-Pharr, Robert F. "Dinge." *Queer Acts*. Ed. José Esteban Muñoz and Amanda Barrett. Special issue of *Women and Performance* 16 (8.2; 1996): 75–85.

"Right to Privacy in Nineteenth-Century America, The." *Harvard Law Review* 94.8 (June 1981): 1892–1910.

Robbins, Bruce. "The Public As Phantom." Introduction to *The Phantom Public Sphere*. Ed. Robbins for the Social Text Collective. Cultural Politics 5. Minneapolis: University of Minnesota Press, 1993. vii–xxvi.

Roberts, Sam. "Their Own Paper Gives Homeless Money and More." *New York Times* 8 January 1990: B1.

Rodgers, Bruce. *The Queens' Vernacular: A Gay Lexicon*. San Francisco: Straight Arrow Books, 1972.

Rohter, Larry. "Pee-wee Herman Enters a Plea of No Contest." *New York Times* 8 November 1991: A12.

Saks, Eva. "Representing Miscegenation Law." *Raritan* 8.2 (Fall 1988): 39–69.

Samar, Vincent J. *The Right to Privacy: Gays, Lesbians, and the Constitution*. Philadelphia: Temple University Press, 1991.

Schmitz, Dawn. "Kowalski and Thompson win!" *Gay Community News* 19.23 (22 December 1991–4 January 1992): 1, 6, 12.

Scott, Darieck. "Jungle Fever? Black Gay Identity Politics, White Dick, and the Utopian Bedroom." *GLQ: A Journal of Lesbian and Gay Studies* 1.3 (1994): 299–321.

Sedgwick, Eve Kosofsky. "Queer and Now." *Tendencies*. Series Q. Durham, N.C.: Duke University Press, 1993. 1–20.

———. "Queer Performativity: Henry James's *The Art of the Novel*." *GLQ: A Journal of Lesbian and Gay Studies* 1.1 (1993): 1–16.

Sims, Calvin. "Subway Peddler Ouster Cheered and Jeered." *New York Times* 18 April 1991: B1.

Sporkin, Elizabeth, with Andrew Abrahams and Don Sider. "Pee-wee's Big Disgrace." *People Weekly* 12 August 1991: 67–70.

Street News (New York City) Fall 1995.

Sullivan, Andrew. *Virtually Normal: An Argument about Homosexuality*. 1995. New York: Vintage, 1996.

———. "When Plagues End: Notes on the Twilight of an Epidemic." *New York Times Magazine* 10 November 1996: 52–62+.

Teltsch, Kathleen. "Editor of Street News Steps Down." *New York Times* 10 June 1990: section 1, p. 36.

———. "Tabloid Sold by the Homeless Is in Trouble." *New York Times* 24 May 1990: B1.

Treichler, Paula A. "AIDS, Homophobia, and Biomedical Discourse: An Epidemic of Signification." Crimp, *AIDS* 31–70.

Tuhkanen, Mikko. "Homoness/Homelessness: Sexuality and Community in Samuel R. Delany's *The Mad Man*." "Homo Academicus: Gay, Lesbian, and Queer Research Seminar." University of Turku, Finland, 9–10 October 1998.

Vecsey, George. "Sports of the Times: Strawberry: One Kiss, One Homer." *New York Times* 5 March 1989: section 8, p. 2.

Wald, Priscilla. "Minefields and Meeting Grounds: Transnational Analyses and American Studies." *American Literary History* 10.1 (Spring 1998): 199–218.

Walker, Adrian. "Boston Diary: Spare Change for Sale." *Boston Globe* 6 April 1992: 21–22.

Walters, Laurel Shaper. "'Spare Change' Helps Homeless." *Christian Science Monitor* 4 June 1992: 12.

Warner, Michael, ed. for the Social Text Collective. *Fear of a Queer Planet: Queer Politics and Social Theory*. Cultural Politics 6. Minneapolis: University of Minnesota Press, 1993.

Warren, Samuel D., and Louis D. Brandeis. "The Right to Privacy." *Harvard Law Review* 4.5 (15 December 1890): 193–220.

Whitford, Frank. *Klimt*. World of Art. London and New York: Thames and Hudson, 1990.

Wilkinson, Peter. "Who Killed Pee-wee Herman?" *Rolling Stone* 3 October 1991: 36–42, 140.

Williams, Margery. *The Velveteen Rabbit; or, How Toys Become Real.* 1922. Illus. William Nicholson. New York: Avon, 1975.

Williams, Patricia J. "On Being the Object of Property." *The Alchemy of Race and Rights.* Cambridge: Harvard University Press, 1991. 216–36.

Williams, Raymond. "Structures of Feeling." *Marxism and Literature.* Marxist Introductions. Oxford: Oxford University Press, 1977. 128–35.

Index

Page numbers in *italics* indicate illustrations.

ABOUT THE AUTHOR

Phillip Brian Harper, Professor of English and American Studies at New York University, is the author of *Framing the Margins: The Social Logic of Postmodern Culture* (1994) and *Are We Not Men? Masculine Anxiety and the Problem of African-American Identity* (1996).